Annual Report of the Council of Inspectors General on Financial Oversight

JULY 2011

Message from the CIGFO Chair

On July 21, 2010, President Obama signed into law the Dodd-Frank Wall Street Reform and Consumer Protection Act, creating the Council of Inspectors General on Financial Oversight (CIGFO). The Council, which includes the Inspectors General of nine major government financial entities, was established to facilitate information sharing among the IG members, provide a forum for discussion of IG member work as it relates to the broader financial sector, and evaluate the effectiveness and internal operations of the Financial Stability Oversight Council (FSOC). Chaired by Treasury Secretary Tim Geithner, the FSOC, also created by the Dodd-Frank Act, is charged with identifying threats to the financial stability of the country, promoting market discipline and responding to emerging risks to the stability of the nation's financial system.

During this first year, both the CIGFO and the FSOC have primarily focused on standing up their respective organizations and developing procedures for conducting business. At the invitation of Chairman Geithner, I attended the FSOC meeting on March 27, 2011, to discuss the CIGFO's oversight role. In addition, I have received regular briefings on FSOC's activities to date.

As FSOC transitions during the next year from a start up to a fully functioning organization, CIGFO will also transition as we fulfill our statutory role of overseeing their work. We expect to establish one or more working groups to conduct audits of FSOC's work, including their process for designating systemically important financial institutions for heightened prudential supervision. As warranted, we would also expect to conduct necessary criminal investigations.

This first CIGFO Annual Report includes a discussion of current and pending joint projects of CIGFO members and an overview of FSOC's compliance with statutory requirements. We find that FSOC has either met or is on target to meet all requirements to date. In addition, our report includes sections, developed by each IG and under his or her exclusive editorial control, that establish a baseline of oversight activity conducted by each IG from the beginning of the current financial crisis through July 14, 2011.

Going forward, we believe that the CIGFO will play a significant role in reviewing FSOC's adherence to the policies and regulations that are currently being put in place and better enable FSOC to meet their goal of comprehensive monitoring to ensure the stability of our nation's financial system.

Eric M. Thorson
Chair, Council of Inspectors General on Financial Oversight
Inspector General, Department of the Treasury

Table of Contents

The Council of Inspectors General on Financial Oversight

The Council of Inspectors General on Financial Oversight (CIGFO) was established by the Dodd-Frank Wall Street Reform and Consumer Protection Act (Dodd-Frank Act) to facilitate sharing of information among CIGFO member Inspectors General (IGs) and to discuss ongoing work of each IG member as it applies to the broader financial sector and ways to improve financial oversight. In addition, the CIGFO may convene working groups to evaluate the effectiveness and internal operations of the Financial Stability Oversight Council (FSOC). Chaired by the IG of the Department of the Treasury (Treasury), the CIGFO is required to meet at least once each quarter.

The CIGFO convened its initial meeting on October 21, 2010 during which it approved a charter (see appendix A) and elected the IG of the Board of Governors of the Federal Reserve System (FRB) as Vice Chair.[1] During the initial meeting, the IGs were briefed by congressional staff regarding the congressional intent in establishing CIGFO and by staff of the FSOC. Subsequent meetings were held on November 30, 2010, February 3, 2011, and May 26, 2011.

Since its initial meeting, the CIGFO has regularly received briefings on actions taken by the FSOC in standing up the Council and initiating rulemaking to meet statutory requirements. A key focus of this oversight has been the FSOC work to develop specific criteria and an analytical framework for designating systemically important financial institutions (SIFIs) for heightened prudential supervision by the FRB.

CIGFO also has a statutory requirement to produce an annual report that includes a section of individual reports under the "exclusive editorial control" of each CIGFO member highlighting concerns and recommendations that may apply to the broader financial sector. The annual report must also include a summary of general observations of CIGFO members focusing on measures that should be taken to improve financial oversight.

CIGFO Membership

- Inspector General of the Board of Governors of the Federal Reserve System
- Inspector General of the Commodity Futures Trading Commission
- Inspector General of the Department of Housing and Urban Development
- Inspector General of the Department of the Treasury, Chair
- Inspector General of the Federal Deposit Insurance Corporation
- Inspector General of the Federal Housing Finance Agency
- Inspector General of the National Credit Union Administration
- Inspector General of the Securities and Exchange Commission
- Special Inspector General for the Troubled Asset Relief Program
  (until termination of authority)

---

1   Following the retirement of the FRB IG, the CIGFO elected the IG of the Federal Deposit insurance Corporation (FDIC) as Vice Chair on May 26, 2011.

Current and Pending Joint Projects

CIGFO member IGs from the Federal Deposit Insurance Corporation (FDIC), FRB and the Department of the Treasury (Treasury) are currently conducting a joint evaluation of prompt regulatory action (PRA) as required by the 1991 amendments to the Federal Deposit Insurance Act (FDIA). The law requires regulators to take action when an institution fails to meet minimum capital levels (Section 38 of FDIA, Prompt Corrective Action) or safety and soundness standards (Section 39 of FDIA, Standards for Safety and Soundness). Over a four-year period, nearly 500 banks triggered prompt corrective action (PCA), including nearly 200 that failed. The joint evaluation will determine the purpose of and circumstances that led to the PRA provisions, evaluate how regulators used the PRA provisions during the economic crisis, assess whether the PRA provisions prompted regulators to act more quickly and forcefully, and determine if other non-capital measures can enhance detection of risks to the Deposit Insurance Fund. The joint project is being coordinated with the Government Accountability Office. A final report is expected to be issued in late summer.

The CIGFO member IGs from the FRB, the Securities and Exchange Commission (SEC), the Commodity Futures Trading Commission (CFTC), the FDIC and Treasury were asked by the Ranking Member and others of the Senate Committee on Banking, Housing, and Urban Affairs to initiate reviews of the economic analysis performed by the regulatory agency under their respective supervision in response to the Dodd-Frank Act. These IGs were also asked to make recommendations on how to improve the rigor and consistency of the agency's economic analysis. Individual reports were issued by June 13, 2011, and many are summarized in the individual IG sections of this CIGFO Annual Report. Discussion of these reviews is planned for a future CIGFO meeting.

The FDIA, as amended, requires that the IG of the appropriate federal banking agency review and report to that agency when an institution under its supervision fails and that failure results in a material loss to the DIF. OIGs from FRB, Treasury, and FDIC continue to work on Material Loss Reviews (MLRs) of banks that failed during the economic crisis. Likewise, the Federal Credit Union Act, as amended, requires the National Credit Union Administration (NCUA) IG to conduct an MLR of a federally insured credit union when there is a material loss to the National Credit Union Share Insurance Fund (NCUSIF). The NCUA OIG is actively engaged in conducting MLRs where there were material losses to the NCUSIF.

During its February 3, 2011 meeting, the CIGFO approved guidelines for the establishment and procedures of working groups. The CIGFO anticipates that, once the FSOC has finalized its rule on designating SIFIs for heightened prudential supervision by the FRB, a working group will be established to oversee the designation process. Other working groups will be considered on an as-needed basis.

Financial Stability Oversight Council Compliance with Statutory Requirements[2]

As established under the Dodd-Frank Act, the FSOC is charged with identifying risks to the financial stability of the United States; promoting market discipline; and responding to emerging threats to the stability of the United States financial system. The FSOC has statutory responsibility to meet at least quarterly, conduct and publish certain studies, and provide an annual report to the Congress. In addition, the FSOC has authority to require supervision and regulation of certain non-bank financial companies; financial market utilities; and payment, clearing, and settlement activities.

To date, the FSOC has met the requirement for quarterly meetings by holding meetings on October 1, 2010, November 23, 2010, January 18, 2011, March 17, 2011, and May 24, 2011. The FSOC Annual Report is on target for publication in summer 2011.

Required FSOC studies include:

Limits on Proprietary Trading and Private Equity/Hedge Fund Sponsorship and Investments (Volcker Rule) Study -- due January 21, 2011

- Notice and Request for Information Regarding the FSOC Volcker Rule Study and Recommendations published October 1, 2010

- FSOC's Study and Recommendations published January 18, 2011

Concentration Limit on Large Companies -- due January 21, 2011

- FSOC's Report on the Concentration Limit on Large Financial Companies published January 18, 2011

Evaluating the Importance of Maximizing U.S. Taxpayer Protections and Promoting Market Discipline to the Treatment of Fully Secured Creditors in the Utilization of the Orderly Liquidation Authority -- due July 21, 2011

- On track for publication in summer 2011

Feasibility, Benefits, Costs and Structure of a Contingent Capital Requirement for Nonbank Financial Companies -- due July 21, 2012

- On track for publication by due date

In exercising its authority to require supervision and regulation of non-bank financial institutions, FSOC has:

- Published on October 1, 2010 an Advanced Notice of Proposed Rulemaking (ANPR)

- Published on January 18, 2011 a Notice of Proposed Rulemaking (NPR)

After the review of extensive public comments and congressional testimony, the FSOC is currently reworking the proposed regulations to provide greater detail. The FSOC plans to seek additional public comment prior to publishing a final rule. In addition, on March 17, 2011, the FSOC published an NPR regarding designations of financial market utilities for heightened supervision.

---

2   Congressional staff requested inclusion of this information in the CIGFO Annual Report. The information was compiled by the CIGFO staff in consultation with the FSOC staff.

Individual Reports of CIGFO-Member Inspectors General

Since the passage of the Dodd Frank Act, steps have been taken to establish both the FSOC and the CIGFO. Under the leadership of the Treasury IG, CIGFO provides an opportunity to leverage the expertise and experience of its IG members, who bring unique independent perspectives to the table and provide collective and individual views through both joint projects and single efforts.

As required by Public Law 111-203, the CIGFO Annual Report must include:

For each inspector general who is a member of the Council of Inspectors General, a section within the exclusive editorial control of such inspector general that highlights the concerns and recommendations of such inspector general in such inspector general's ongoing and completed work, with a focus on issues that may apply to the broader financial sector.

This section includes reports from:

- Inspector General of the Board of Governors of the Federal Reserve System
- Inspector General of the Commodity Futures Trading Commission
- Inspector General of the Department of Housing and Urban Development
- Inspector General of the Department of the Treasury
- Inspector General of the Federal Deposit Insurance Corporation
- Inspector General of the Federal Housing Finance Agency
- Inspector General of the National Credit Union Administration
- Inspector General of the Securities and Exchange Commission
- Special Inspector General of the Troubled Asset Relief Program

This first report highlights the selected efforts of each IG on the CIGFO over the past two-plus years as they relate to issues impacting the broader financial sector and financial oversight. The work presented in these individual reports was not conducted under the auspices of CIGFO but, rather, represents completed or ongoing work on issues of mutual interest or concern, as well as important bodies of work specific to each IG's respective agency.

Office of Inspector General
Board of Governors of the Federal Reserve System
and Bureau of Consumer Financial Protection

Background

With the enactment of the Inspector General Act Amendments of 1988, Congress established the Office of Inspector General (OIG) as an independent oversight authority for the newly established Board of Governors of the Federal Reserve System (Board)—the government agency component of the broader Federal Reserve System. In addition, on July 21, 2010, the Dodd-Frank Wall Street Reform and Consumer Protection Act (Dodd-Frank Act) statutorily established the OIG as the independent oversight authority for the Bureau of Consumer Financial Protection (Bureau).

Under the authority of the Inspector General Act of 1978, as amended (IG Act), the OIG conducts independent and objective audits, inspections, evaluations, investigations, and other reviews related to the programs and operations of the Board and the Bureau. Through its work, the OIG promotes integrity, economy, efficiency, and effectiveness; helps prevent and detect fraud, waste, and abuse; and strengthens the agencies' accountability to Congress and the public.

Through its independent oversight, the OIG supports

- the Board in fostering the stability, integrity, and efficiency of the nation's monetary, financial, and payment systems to promote optimal macroeconomic performance; and

- the Bureau in implementing and enforcing federal consumer financial law to ensure that consumers have access to fair, transparent, and competitive financial markets, products, and services.

In addition to the duties set forth in the IG Act, Congress has mandated additional responsibilities for the OIG. Section 38(k) of the Federal Deposit Insurance Act (FDI Act) requires that the OIG review failed financial institutions supervised by the Board that result in a material loss to the Deposit Insurance Fund (DIF) and produce a report within six months. The Dodd-Frank Act amended section 38(k) of the FDI Act by raising the materiality threshold, but also required the OIG to report on the results of any nonmaterial losses to the DIF that exhibited unusual circumstances warranting an in-depth review.

In addition, section 211(f) of the Dodd-Frank Act requires that the OIG review the Board's supervision of any covered financial company that is placed into receivership. The OIG will produce a report that evaluates the effectiveness of the Board's supervision, identifies any acts or omissions by the Board that contributed to or could have prevented the company's receivership status, and recommends appropriate administrative or legislation action.

Section 11B of the Federal Reserve Act mandates annual independent audits of the financial statements of each Federal Reserve Bank and of the Board. Our office oversees the annual financial statement audits of the Board, as well as the Federal Financial Institutions Examination Council (FFIEC). The FFIEC is a formal interagency body empowered to prescribe uniform principles, standards, and report forms for the federal examination of financial institutions by the Board, the Federal Deposit Insurance Corporation (FDIC), the National Credit Union Administration (NCUA), the Office of the Comptroller of the Currency (OCC), and the Office of Thrift Supervision (OTS) and to make recommendations to promote uniformity in the supervision of financial institutions.

With respect to information technology, the Federal Information Security Management Act of 2002 (FISMA) established a legislative mandate for ensuring the effectiveness of information security controls over resources that support federal operations and assets. Consistent with FISMA's requirements, our office performs an annual independent evaluation of the Board's information security program and practices, including the effectiveness of security controls and techniques for selected information systems. Our office also will conduct an annual independent evaluation of the Bureau's information security program and practices once the Bureau is fully operational.

OIG Reports and Other Products Related to the Broader Financial Sector

In accordance with section 989E(A)(2)(B) of the Dodd-Frank Act, the following highlights the ongoing and completed work of our office, with a focus on issues that may apply to the broader financial sector.

Ongoing Work

Review of the Board's Process to Manage the Implementation of the Dodd-Frank Act

Given the significance of the Dodd-Frank Act, our office is conducting an *Audit of the Implementation of the Dodd-Frank Wall Street Reform and Consumer Protection Act*. The Dodd-Frank Act established numerous requirements for the Board and other financial regulatory agencies and created the Financial Stability Oversight Council (FSOC) to enhance oversight across the financial sector. In addition to meeting a variety of new responsibilities under the act, the Board must draft a number of new regulations, review existing regulations and policies, and conduct various studies. For many of these initiatives, the Dodd-Frank Act specifies deadlines for final actions over a 30-month period following the act's enactment.

Our audit objectives are to assess (1) the efficiency and effectiveness of the Board's processes for identifying, tracking, and overall managing its responsibilities under the act; and (2) the Board's progress in implementing key requirements of the act.

Review of the Implementation Planning Activities of the Bureau

Since the Dodd-Frank Act authorizes the Secretary of the Treasury to perform certain Bureau functions until a Director is in place, our office currently shares joint oversight responsibility for the Bureau with the OIG of the Department of the Treasury (Treasury). As part of this joint oversight responsibility, our offices initiated an evaluation to assess the Bureau's development and execution of an implementation plan and timeline to establish the agency's functions. The objectives are to evaluate the Bureau's efforts to (1) identify mission-critical activities and legislative mandates; (2) develop and execute a comprehensive implementation plan and timeline for mission-critical activities and legislative mandates; and (3) communicate its implementation plan and timeline to key stakeholders.

Audit of the Board's Progress in Developing Enhanced Prudential Standards and Monitoring of Potential Systemic Risks

We have also begun an audit of the Board's Division of Banking Supervision and Regulation's (BS&R's) implementation of certain provisions of the Dodd-Frank Act. The Dodd-Frank Act gave the Board important new authorities to safeguard financial stability, including the responsibility for developing enhanced prudential standards for supervising large bank holding companies with total consolidated assets of $50 billion or more and systemically important non-bank financial companies identified by the FSOC. The objectives of this audit are to assess how BS&R is (1) developing enhanced prudential standards for large bank holding companies, including standards that would apply to any non-bank financial company that the FSOC identifies as systemically important; and (2) monitoring potential systemic risk, including emerging mortgage foreclosure-related issues.

Cross-Cutting Review of Failed Banks that Were Supervised by the Board

The OIG is conducting a cross-cutting review of the lessons learned from our cumulative body of reviews of state member bank failures to identify themes related to the causes of the bank failures, and recommend potential improvements in bank supervisory policies and practices. The individual reviews of state member bank failures that comprise this cross-cutting project were required pursuant to section 38(k) of the FDI Act.

Evaluation of Prompt Regulatory Action Provisions of the FDI Act

Our office is working with the OIGs of the FDIC and the Treasury on a joint evaluation of the prompt regulatory action provisions of the FDI Act. The prompt regulatory action provisions of the FDI Act include section 38 (Prompt Corrective Action (PCA)) and section 39 (Standards for Safety and Soundness). In general, these provisions require federal regulators to institute a system of regulatory actions that is triggered when an institution fails to meet minimum capital levels or certain safety and soundness standards. These provisions were intended to increase the likelihood that regulators would respond promptly and forcefully to minimize losses to the DIF when federally insured banks fail. This project is focused on the following objectives:

- Determining the purpose of and circumstances that led to the prompt regulatory action provisions (FDI Act sections 38 and 39) and lessons learned from the savings and loan crisis;

- Evaluating to what extent PCA and the Standards for Safety and Soundness were a factor in bank failures and problem institutions during the current crisis;

- Assessing whether these provisions prompted federal regulators to act more quickly and more forcefully to limit losses to the DIF, in light of findings and lessons learned from the savings and loan crisis and regulators' use of prompt regulatory action provisions in the current crisis; and

- Determining whether there are other non-capital measures that provide a leading indication of risks to the DIF that should be considered as part of the prompt regulatory action provisions.

Completed Work

Review of the Federal Reserve's Section 13(3) Lending Facilities to Support Overall Market Liquidity: Function, Status, and Risk Management

In response to the financial crisis and to avoid systemic financial failure within the U. S. economy, between March and November 2008, the Board, citing "unusual and exigent circumstances," exercised its authority under section 13(3) of the Federal Reserve Act to authorize the creation of six lending facilities to support overall market liquidity: the Term Securities Lending Facility (TSLF) (including the TSLF Options Program), the Primary Dealer Credit Facility (PDCF), the Asset-Backed Commercial Paper Money Market Mutual Fund Liquidity Facility (AMLF), the Commercial Paper Funding Facility (CPFF), the Money Market Investor Funding Facility (MMIFF), and the Term Asset-Backed Securities Loan Facility (TALF). These lending programs were intended to stabilize commercial paper, asset-backed securities, repurchase agreements, money market, and other financial markets. The combined usage of the six facilities peaked at $600 billion on November 5, 2008.

Our office's review (1) analyzed the overall function and status of each lending facility, including how it operated, the financial markets it was intended to support, and the financial utilization of the facility, and (2) identified credit and operational risks and controls in each lending facility. The results were for the Board's review in exercising its monetary policy function and its general supervision and oversight of the Federal Reserve Banks. The lending facilities included credit risks based on the broad eligibility for borrowers, the non-recourse nature of some of the lending facilities' loans, and the potential aggregate exposure to certain types of collateral and various types of borrowers. The lending facilities also included operational risks associated with developing and maintaining policies and procedures; having sufficient, experienced staff to run the facilities; and managing vendor contracts and agent agreements. The Federal Reserve took various actions to mitigate risk, including, in most cases, a haircut on the collateral, imposing above-normal market interest rates and usage fees, contracting with specialized vendors for critical functions, borrowing staff from other sections of the Federal Reserve Bank, hiring some additional staff, performing on-site reviews of vendors' and agents' compliance with contract and agreement provisions, and establishing contractual conflict of interest provisions.

Overall, general indicators of market stress suggested that the lending facilities helped to stabilize the commercial paper, asset-backed securities, repurchase agreements, money market, and other financial markets. As of the end of our fieldwork in June 2010, the Board reported that none of the lending facilities had experienced any financial losses. Each of the six lending facilities has expired, as market conditions have improved. As of June 2010, the lending facilities had generated approximately $9.0 billion in interest earnings and fees. Our office performed this work to provide an independent review of the six lending facilities' functions, status, and risks. Our report did not include any recommendations.

Congressional Request to Review the Economic Analysis Associated with Five Rules Required under the Dodd-Frank Act

On May 4, 2011, the OIGs for the Board, the Treasury, the FDIC, the Commodity Futures Trading Commission, and the Securities and Exchange Commission received a request from the minority members of the Senate Committee on Banking, Housing, and Urban Affairs to review the economic analysis performed for certain proposed rules required under the Dodd-Frank Act. The request included specific questions related to the proposed rules as well as broader issues associated with the rulemaking process. Our office was asked to focus on five specific rulemakings:

- Credit Risk Retention, 76 FR 24090 (April 29, 2011);

- Risk-Based Capital Standards: Advanced Capital Adequacy Framework-Basel II – Establishment of a Risk-Based Capital Floor, 75 FR 82317 (December 30, 2010);

- Margin and Capital Requirements for Covered Swap Entities, 76 FR 27564 (May 11, 2011);

- Regulation Z; Truth in Lending Act, 76 FR 27390 (May 11, 2011); and

- Financial Market Utilities, 76 FR 18445 (April 4, 2011).

To answer the questions included in the Committee Members' letter, we reviewed documentation from each of the rulemaking teams, including materials related to economic analysis that was performed, and interviewed over 30 Board staff members who worked on each of the selected proposed rulemaking teams.

Our June 13, 2011, report noted that a number of key statutes related to the Board's regulatory authority generally do not require economic analysis as part of the agency's rulemaking activities. While the Dodd-Frank Act does not contain a general provision requiring economic analysis as part of every rulemaking or explicitly require that an "economic analysis" or "cost-benefit analysis" support any of the five rules that we reviewed, we found that the statute identifies certain considerations, assessments, policy goals, or substantive requirements that must be reflected in the applicable proposed rule.

We reported that the Board is subject to, among other things, the Paperwork Reduction Act (PRA), and the Regulatory Flexibility Act (RFA). Our review indicated that the Board complied with the applicable Dodd-Frank Act statutory requirements for the respective rulemakings and also complied with the PRA and the RFA. With respect to Executive Orders 12866 and 13563, our analysis determined that the requirements outlined in Executive Order 12866 generally do not apply to the Board because the order exempts independent regulatory agencies such as the Board. Likewise, Executive Order 13563 also generally does not apply to the Board because the order does not alter terms previously defined in Executive Order 12866.

We found that the applicable laws, regulations, executive orders, and relevant guidance did not require that any of the five rulemakings include a macro-level cost-benefit assessment related to the rulemaking, or require an assessment of the five rules' impact on job creation or economic growth. However, documentation we reviewed indicated that the Board conducts the quantitative economic analysis necessary to satisfy statutory requirements, including "consideration" requirements; and, on a discretionary basis, the Board also conducts the quantitative economic analysis it deems necessary to support the rulemaking.

We noted that the Board's Rulemaking Procedures Policy Statement was out of date, and we recommended that it be updated and disseminated to all employees involved in rulemaking activities. We also recommended that the Board consider establishing internal documentation standards for rulemaking economic analysis to help ensure reproducibility on an internal basis.

Audit of the Board's Processing of Applications for the Capital Purchase Program under the Troubled Asset Relief Program

The Emergency Economic Stabilization Act of 2008, Public Law No. 110-343, authorized the Troubled Asset Relief Program (TARP). Under the TARP's Capital Purchase Program (CPP), the Treasury was authorized to fund qualified financial institutions with up to $250 billion of capital through the purchase of preferred shares or senior securities of the qualifying institutions. In general, financial institutions requested participation in the CPP by submitting an application to the appropriate federal banking agency, which reviewed the application and made a recommendation to Treasury on whether a CPP request should be approved or denied.

Our office assessed the Board's process and controls for reviewing CPP applications from Board-supervised financial institutions seeking to participate in the CPP. Overall, we found that the Board's limited procedures were consistent with Treasury's guidance for reviewing applications and making recommendations for funding. In addition, we found that the Board's recommendations to Treasury for approval of applications generally reflected compliance with Treasury's guidance and the Board's internal procedures. Our testing identified some compliance deficiencies, such as incomplete documentation on analysis of the institutions' capital, asset quality, earnings, and liquidity; missing quality assurance certifications by Reserve Bank senior officials; and a lack of documentation on analysis of institutions' ongoing viability. However, due to compensating controls at the Board, we did not identify any instances where these deficiencies led to approval of financial institutions that did not meet eligibility criteria or that otherwise should not have been approved.

Specifically, we found that the Board received limited guidance from Treasury in the early stages of the CPP program regarding what analysis should be performed to determine the viability of the financial institutions. As the Board began reviewing applications under the limited guidance, Board officials raised issues to Treasury officials that resulted in additional Treasury guidance. The Board sent email messages to the Reserve Banks outlining procedures for processing the applications and additional analysis to be performed in reviewing the applications. Although not required by Treasury, we believe that formal, detailed and documented procedures would have provided the Board and the Reserve Banks additional assurance of consistently and completely analyzing CPP applications. Our report included a recommendation that, as the CPP application phase drew down and the Board moved forward with analyzing redemption requests from CPP-funded institutions, the Board incorporate lessons learned from the CPP application review process to help ensure that a complete, formal, and documented set of procedures was implemented and followed to further the consistent and thorough analysis of redemption requests.

We also found that, while the Board had established tracking systems to document outside contacts regarding the CPP program and the Board's responses, CPP-related communications between Reserve Bank staffs and institutions had not been documented and tracked. While we did not identify any improper communications, our report included a recommendation that the Board develop a case tracking system to document relevant communications between Reserve Bank staff and institutions regarding their CPP applications and redemption requests.

Joint Response by the OIGs of the Treasury and the Board to a Congressional Request for Information Concerning the Bureau of Consumer Financial Protection

On January 10, 2011, the Board and the Treasury OIGs jointly issued a letter that responded to a November 22, 2010, congressional request for information related to the Bureau's transparency, organizational structure, and regulatory agenda. In order to respond, we (1) reviewed the applicable sections of the Dodd-Frank Act and other relevant laws, (2) requested, obtained, and reviewed relevant information and documentation from the Board and the Treasury, and (3) interviewed key Treasury officials.

As noted in our letter, Secretary of the Treasury Timothy Geithner delegated his interim authority to establish the Bureau to Professor Elizabeth Warren and other Treasury officials. Professor Warren is the Assistant to the President and Special Advisor to the Secretary of the Treasury on the Consumer Financial Protection Bureau. According to Treasury, Professor Warren's implementation activities are overseen by Secretary Geithner, and she has regular meetings with senior Treasury officials regarding the status of start-up efforts and the priorities she has identified for the Bureau.

Our response noted that Treasury implemented a policy to disclose meetings regarding Bureau-related activities between senior Treasury officials, including Professor Warren, and individuals from private sector entities. In addition, Treasury noted that Professor Warren's schedule had been, and would continue to be, posted on its website.

With respect to organizational structure, our response indicated that the Bureau had prepared a draft organizational plan. The response also included, as requested, the names of Treasury and Board employees and detailees in certain specified categories of positions, such as members of the Senior Executive Service, who were working to build the Bureau's infrastructure. To support implementation activities, the Bureau requested and received from the Board nearly $33 million. With regard to the regulatory agenda, Professor Warren provided examples of two policy initiatives that will receive priority: (1) consolidating duplicative and overlapping mortgage disclosure forms mandated by the Truth in Lending Act and the Real Estate Settlement Procedures Act and (2) simplifying credit card agreements to ensure that customers fully understand fees and finance charges.

Finally, our response indicated that Treasury's interim authority extends beyond the designated transfer date if the Bureau does not have its Director in place at that time. After the July 21, 2011, designated transfer date and until the Director is confirmed, the Treasury Secretary has the authority to carry out certain functions of the Bureau, which include prescribing rules, conducting examinations, and enforcing orders. Treasury cannot, however, exercise the certain newly established authorities, which include prohibiting unfair, deceptive, or abusive acts or practices.

In addition to our January 10, 2011, response, OIG staff provided two oral briefings to staff members of representatives on the House Committee on Financial Services. We also issued a follow-up letter on March 15, 2011, that included the names of employees in certain specified categories of positions from federal agencies other than the Board and the Treasury who performed tasks related to establishing the Bureau. The Department of Housing and Urban Development, the FDIC, the OCC, the OTS, the NCUA, and the Federal Trade Commission provided us the names of more than 100 employees who were working in various capacities to facilitate the transfer of their organizations' functions to the Bureau.

Review of the Joint Implementation Plan for the Transfer of OTS Functions

Title III of the Dodd-Frank Act established provisions for the transfer of power and authority of the OTS to the OCC, the FDIC, and the Board within one year after enactment of the Act (by July 21, 2011). Under Title III, the Board will receive the functions and rulemaking authority for consolidated supervision of savings and loan holding companies and their non-depository subsidiaries.

The Dodd-Frank Act required that, within 180 days after its enactment, the OTS, the OCC, the FDIC, and the Board jointly submit a plan (Joint Implementation Plan) to Congress and the Inspectors General of the Treasury, the FDIC, and the Board (Inspectors General) that detailed the steps each agency would take to implement the Title III provisions. The Joint Implementation Plan was issued to Congress and the Inspectors General on January 25, 2011. The Dodd-Frank Act required that the Inspectors General conduct an audit to determine whether the implementation plan conformed to the Title III provisions and issue a report within 60 days after the submission of the Joint Implementation Plan.

On March 28, 2011, the Inspectors General jointly issued a report concluding that the actions in the Joint Implementation Plan generally conformed to the provisions of Title III. The report stated that the Board's component of the implementation plan sufficiently addressed the applicable Title III requirements. However, the report (1) noted that the Joint Implementation Plan did not address the prohibition against involuntary separation or relocation of transferred OTS employees for 30 months (except under certain circumstances), and (2) recommended that the Joint Implementation Plan be amended to address this requirement.

In accordance with the Dodd-Frank Act, the Inspectors General will jointly provide a status report on the progress of the Joint Implementation Plan every six months until all aspects of the plan have been implemented.

Office of Inspector General
Commodity Futures Trading Commission

Background

The CFTC OIG was created in 1989 in accordance with the 1988 amendments to the Inspector General Act of 1978 (P.L. 95-452). OIG was established as an independent unit to:

- promote economy, efficiency and effectiveness in the administration of CFTC programs and operations and detect and prevent fraud, waste and abuse in such programs and operations;

- conduct and supervise audits and, where necessary, investigations relating to the administration of CFTC programs and operations;

- review existing and proposed legislation, regulations and exchange rules and make recommendations concerning their impact on the economy and efficiency of CFTC programs and operations or the prevention and detection of fraud and abuse;

- recommend policies for, and conduct, supervise, or coordinate other activities carried out or financed by such establishment for the purpose of promoting economy and efficiency in the administration of, or preventing and detecting fraud and abuse in, its programs and operations;

- and keep the Commission and Congress fully informed about any problems or deficiencies in the administration of CFTC programs and operations and provide recommendations for correction of these problems or deficiencies.

CFTC OIG operates independently of the Agency and has not experienced any interference from the CFTC Chairman in connection with the conduct of any investigation, inspection, evaluation, review, or audit, and our investigations have been pursued regardless of the rank or party affiliation of the target.[3]

Role in Financial Oversight

The CFTC OIG has no direct statutory duties related to oversight of the futures, swaps and derivatives markets; rather, the CFTC OIG acts as an independent Office within the CFTC that conducts investigations, reviews, inspections, and other activities designed to identify fraud, waste, and abuse in connection with CFTC programs and operations, and makes recommendations and referrals as appropriate. The CFTC's yearly financial statement audit is conducted by the independent public accounting firm of KPMG.

---

3   The Inspector General Act of 1978, as amended, states: "Neither the head of the establishment nor the officer next in rank below such head shall prevent or prohibit the Inspector General from initiating, carrying out, or completing any audit or investigation...." 5 U.S.C. App. 3 sec. 3(a).

Recent, Current or Ongoing Work in Financial Oversight

An Investigation Regarding Cost-Benefit Analyses Performed by the Commodity Futures Trading Commission in connection with Rulemakings Undertaken Pursuant to the Dodd-Frank Act

In April 2011, the Office of the Inspector General for the Commodity Futures Trading Commission completed a report[4] addressing the formulation of cost benefit analyses for four separate rulemakings recently published by the Commodity Futures Trading Commission in accordance with the Dodd-Frank Act:[5]

> Further Defining "Swap Dealer," "Security-based Swap Dealer," "Major Swap Participant," "Major Security-based Swap Participant," and "Eligible Contract Participant," 75 FR 80174 (December 21, 2010) (Joint proposed rule; proposed interpretations);6

> Confirmation, Portfolio Reconciliation, Compression Requirements for Swap Dealers and Major Swap Participants, 75 FR 81519 (December 28, 2010) (Notice of proposed rulemaking);

> Core Principles and Other Requirements for Designated Contract Markets, 75 FR 80572 (December 22, 2010) (Notice of proposed rulemaking);

> Regulations Establishing and Governing the Duties of Swap Dealers and Major Swap Participants, 75 FR 71397 (November 23, 2010) (Notice of proposed rulemaking).

We undertook this investigation at the request of Representative Frank D. Lucas, Chairman, House Committee on Agriculture, and Representative K. Michael Conaway, Chairman, Subcommittee on General Farm Commodities and Risk.[7] We were asked to review eight factors in our investigation, and were requested to complete our investigation by April 15, 2011.

In order to complete the investigation, we reviewed drafts of the cost-benefit analyses for the four proposed rules, staff email, and internal memoranda. In addition, we conducted interviews with 24 CFTC employees at staff and various management levels who were involved (or were reported to us as involved) with the cost-benefit analysis processes for the four rules.

The cost-benefit analyses were created as follows. Following enactment of the Dodd-Frank Act,[8] the Chairman and Division Directors created 30 rulemaking teams.[9] Because section 15(a) of the Commodity Exchange Act (the Act)[10] required the consideration of a cost-benefit analysis for each rulemaking, the Office

---

4   http://www.cftc.gov/ucm/groups/public/@aboutcftc/documents/file/oig_investigationreport.pdf.

5   Dodd-Frank Wall Street Reform and Consumer Protection Act, Public Law 111-203, 124 Stat. 1376 (2010) ("Dodd-Frank Act" or "Dodd-Frank").

6   The Commission published this proposed rule jointly with the Securities and Exchange Commission, in consultation with the Board of Governors of the Federal Reserve System. 75 FR 80174 (December 21, 2010).

7   The request is available here: http://agriculture.house.gov/pdf/letters/cftc_inspectorgeneral110311.pdf

8   Dodd-Frank Wall Street Reform and Consumer Protection Act, Public Law 111-203, 124 Stat. 1376 (2010) ("Dodd-Frank Act" or "Dodd-Frank").

9   A 31st team was later created and tasked with developing conforming rules to update the CFTC's existing regulations to take into account the provisions of the Act. Testimony of Chairman Gary Gensler before the House Committee on Agriculture, February 10, 2011, available at: http://www.cftc.gov/PressRoom/SpeechesTestimony/opagensler-68.html.

10   7 USC sec. 19.

of General Counsel and Office of Chief Economist created a uniform methodology for cost-benefit analysis for use Agency-wide. That methodology, contained in a September 2010 memo signed by the General Counsel and the Chief Economist, set out in some detail the types of qualitative considerations that might inform a cost-benefit analysis, encouraged the use of both qualitative and quantitative data, and included a template for everyone to follow.

Although the development of a uniform methodology appeared to be an equal effort between the Office of General Counsel and the Office of Chief Economist, in practice the cost-benefit analyses involved less input from the Office of Chief Economist, with the Office of General Counsel taking a dominant role. For the four rules we reviewed, the cost-benefit analyses were drafted by Commission staff in divisions other than the Office of Chief Economist. Staff from the Office of Chief Economist did review the drafts, but their edits were not always accepted.

To a greater or lesser extent for the four examined rules, the Office of General Counsel not only appeared to have the greater "say" in the proposed cost-benefit analyses, they appeared to rely heavily on an historic (and somewhat stripped down) analytical approach. We noted that similar economic analyses in the context of federal rulemaking had proved perilous for financial market regulators.[11] Moreover, a bare bones economic analysis in the context of rulemaking seemed odd for an agency that regularly engages in economic analysis pertaining to the futures markets. We recognized that cost-benefit analysis does not possess anywhere near the exactitude of, say, calculus, but believed it should provide structure for evaluation. A more robust process was clearly permitted under the cost-benefit guidance issued by the Office of General Counsel and the Office of Chief Economist, and we believed a more robust approach would be desirable, with greater input from the Office of Chief Economist. We agreed with a noted commenter that economic analysis in the context of rulemaking, "is more than about satisfying procedural requirements for regulatory rulemaking."[12]

Following release of our report, we learned that the General Counsel and Chief Economist in May 2011 issued detailed guidance for cost-benefit analyses for final rulemakings that appears designed to lead to more robust cost-benefit analyses in the future. In addition, in May 2011, 10 Senators requested a further study on cost-benefit analyses published in connection four additional proposed rules under Dodd-Frank. On June 13, 2011, CFTC OIG issued its second study on cost-benefit analyses published by CFTC in connection with Dodd-Frank rulemakings, analyzing an additional four rules and ultimately reiterating our earlier recommendations.[13]

---

11   See, e.g., Am Equity Investment Life Ins. Co. v. S.E.C., 613 F.3d 166, 177-178 (D.C. Cir.2010); Chamber of Commerce of U.S. v. S.E.C., 412 F.3d 133, 142-144 (D.C. Cir.2005).

12   Testimony of James A. Overdahl, Vice President, National Economic Research Associates, Before the Committee on Financial Services, Subcommittee on Oversight and Investigations, United States House of Representatives March 30, 2011, available at: http://financialservices.house.gov/media/pdf/033011overdahl.pdf.

13   A Review Of Cost-Benefit Analyses Performed by the Commodity Futures Trading Commission in Connection with Rulemakings Undertaken Pursuant to the Dodd-Frank Act. (Available at: http://www.cftc.gov/ucm/groups/public/@ aboutcftc/documents/file/oig_investigation_061311.pdf

Office of Inspector General
Department of Housing and Urban Development

The U.S. Department of Housing and Urban Development (HUD) Inspector General (HUD OIG) is one of the original 12 Inspectors General authorized under the Inspector General Act of 1978. The HUD OIG strives to make a difference in HUD's performance and accountability. HUD OIG has a strong commitment to their statutory mission of detecting and preventing fraud, waste, and abuse, and promoting the effectiveness and efficiency of government operations.

While organizationally located within HUD, the HUD OIG operates independently with separate budget authority. Their independence allows for clear and objective reporting to the Secretary and to the Congress. HUD's primary mission is to improve housing and expand opportunities for families seeking to improve their quality of life. HUD does this through a variety of housing and community development programs aimed at helping Americans nationwide obtain affordable housing. These programs are funded through a $45 billion annual budget and the Federal Housing Administration (FHA) mortgage insurance for Single-Family and Multifamily properties, which is self funded through mortgage insurance premiums.

The past several years have seen enormous and damaging developments in the mortgage market:

- The dissolution of the subprime and Alt-A loan markets;

- Dramatic drops in housing prices in most areas of the country;

- A concomitant rise in default and foreclosures;

- Financial insecurity in the mortgage-backed securities markets represented by the government takeover of Fannie Mae and Freddie Mac;

- The collapse of credit markets; and,

- As a primary vehicle to address these issues, an urgent reliance on the FHA to bolster the mortgage market.

As the Mortgage Asset Research Institute has stated, the unprecedented onslaught of financial losses, reputational damages, and rehabilitative public policies will forever reshape the mortgage industry. While there are other programs at HUD that are being utilized in a significant way to help stimulate the economy (i.e., billions of dollars in new funding to Community Development Block Grants, to increased Public Housing assistance, etc.), which are also vulnerable to fraudulent and abusive activities, our focus has remained steady on the FHA program due to the mortgage crisis and to an increased reliance on our Department to resolve foreclosure matters at this critical juncture.

The current degree of FHA predominance in the market is unparalleled. First off, to put the FHA issues into perspective, we have recently stated in testimony to the Congress that, through the multitude of our work in auditing and investigating many facets of the FHA programs over the course of many years, OIG has had, and continues to have, concerns regarding FHA's systems and infrastructure to adequately perform its current requirements and services. This was expressed by the OIG to the FHA through audits and reports regarding a wide spectrum of areas prior to the current influx of loans coming into the program and prior to the consideration of the numerous proposals that expanded its reach. OIG continues to remain concerned regarding FHA's ability and capacity to oversee the newly generated business.

Some of these are long-standing concerns that go back to unresolved issues highlighted in our work products from as far back as the early to mid-1990's.

The Housing and Economic Recovery Act (HERA), created a new Hope for Homeowners program to enable FHA to refinance the mortgages of at-risk borrowers. While activity to date has been limited, the FHA was authorized to guarantee $300 billion in new loans to help prevent an estimated 400,000 homeowners from foreclosure. While the goal to help homeowners in distress is important, a redraft to relax qualification requirements for borrowers and lenders may create a situation that could be exploited by fraud perpetrators to take advantage of desperate homeowners, at risk-lenders, and the FHA insurance fund. The HERA legislation also authorized changes to the FHA's Home Equity Conversion Mortgage (HECM) program that will enable more seniors to tap into their home's equity and obtain higher payouts which raises new oversight concerns for this agency.

OIG is concerned that increases in demand to the FHA program are having collateral implications for the integrity of the Government National Mortgage Association (Ginnie Mae) mortgage-backed securities (MBS) program including the potential for increases in fraud in that program. Ginnie Mae securities are the only MBS to carry the full faith and credit guaranty of the United States. If an issuer fails to make the required pass-through payment of principal and interest to MBS investors, Ginnie Mae is required to assume responsibility for it. Typically, Ginnie Mae defaults the issuers and assumes control of the issuer's MBS pools. Like FHA, Ginnie Mae has seen an augmentation in its market share. From a different vantage point, the industry has noted that Ginnie Mae's struggle to keep pace with FHA could also reduce liquidity at a critical moment in the housing market.

The OIG has initiated investigations of Ginnie Mae MBS fraud. In one recent case, the two former corporate officers of a Michigan financial company were convicted of defrauding Ginnie Mae by retaining the funds obtained from terminated and/or paid off loans. The defendants failed to disclose to Ginnie Mae that the loans were terminated, while one of the defendants utilized the funds from the paid-off loans to invest in the stock market and to make fraudulent monthly payments to Ginnie Mae on the loans that were previously paid-off in order to conceal the fraud. The fraud began during July of 1998 and continued until October of 2007, resulting in a loss of approximately $20,000,000.

OIG was gratified that a new penalty provision was inserted into the Housing and Economic Recovery Act (now 18 U.S.C. Section 1014). When OIG corresponded during consideration of that legislation, we stated our belief that a new penalty enunciated specifically for the FHA program would be beneficial from an oversight and enforcement perspective. We assisted in its development and were very pleased that it was included in the final passage. The statute now creates a penalty of up to $1 million and 30 years in prison for committing fraud against FHA programs, similar to the predicates established in the Financial Institutions Reform, Recovery and Enforcement Act, and will be a useful tool for prosecutors and the law enforcement community to employ in order to address those who would seek to defraud the program.

A significant problem facing FHA, and the lenders it works with, is the fallout from decreasing home values. This increases the risk of default, abandonment and foreclosure, and makes it correspondingly difficult for FHA to resell the properties. A major cause for concern is that even as FHA endorsement levels meet or exceed previous peaks in its program history, FHA defaults have already exceeded previous years. This reinforces the importance for FHA approved lenders to maintain solid underwriting standards and quality control processes in order to withstand severe adverse economic conditions.

Until recently, FHA's market share remained quite low as conventional subprime loans were heavily marketed by lenders. The tightening credit market has increased FHA's position as a loan insurer and, with that, is coming an increase in lender/brokers seeking to do business with the federal program and an overall concern regarding some of these loan originators.

Many "traditional" fraud schemes continue to affect FHA and are described below:

Appraisal Fraud

Typically central to every loan origination fraud and includes deliberately fraudulent appraisals (substantially misrepresented properties, fictitious properties, bogus comparables) and/or inflated appraisals (designed to "hit the numbers"); appraiser kickbacks; and appraiser coercion.

Identity Theft

Often includes use of bogus, invalid or misused Social Security numbers and may include involvement of illegal aliens, false ownership documents or certifications.

Loan Origination Fraud

Including false, fraudulent and substantially inaccurate income, assets and employment information; false loan applications, false credit letters and reports; false gift letters; seller-funded down payments; concealed cash transactions; straw buyers; flipping; kickbacks; cash-out schemes; fraud rings; and inadequate or fraudulent underwriting activities. While these types of mortgage fraud schemes continue to operate, changing market conditions have generated new or variant schemes.

Rescue or Foreclosure Fraud

Recent trends show that certain individuals in the industry are preying on desperate and vulnerable homeowners who are facing foreclosure. Some improper activities include equity skimming [whereby the homeowner is approached and offered an opportunity to get out of financial trouble by the promise to pay off the mortgage or to receive a sum of money when the property is sold -- the property is then deeded to the unscrupulous individual who may charge the homeowner rent and then fails to make the mortgage payment thereby causing the property to go into foreclosure] and lease/buy-back plans [wherein the homeowner is deceived into signing over title with the belief that they can remain in the house as a renter and eventually buy back -- the terms are so unrealistic that buy-back is impossible and the homeowner loses possession with the new title holder walking away with most or all of the equity].

Bankruptcy Fraud

Typically Chapter 7 bankruptcy petitions are filed in lieu of Chapter 13 petitions on behalf of debtors; however, property sales information is fraudulently withheld from the bankruptcy court and the properties are leased back to the debtors at inflated rents. The debtors' property ownership and equity are stripped from them.

Home Equity Conversion Mortgage (reverse mortgage) Fraud

FHA reverse mortgages are a new and potentially vulnerable area for fraud perpetrators. We are aware that the larger loan limits can be attractive to exploiters of the elderly, whether it is by third parties or by family members, who seek to strip equity from senior homeowners.

The tasks before the HUD OIG are daunting ones: addressing the elements of fraud that were involved in the collapse of the mortgage market; monitoring the roll-out of new FHA loan products in order to reduce exploitation of program vulnerabilities; and, combating perpetrators of fraud, including those who have migrated from the subprime markets, who would exploit FHA loan programs. The consequences of the current mortgage crisis, its worldwide economic implications, and the subsequent pressures placed on the Department and OIG could not have come at a more inopportune time. The Department, as a whole, has had significant new leadership responsibilities over the last seven years in rebuilding communities devastated by disasters (i.e., lower Manhattan post-September 11th; the Gulf Coast region after hurricanes Katrina, Rita and Wilma; the Galveston area after recent hurricanes; California fires; and Midwest flooding) that have added tens of billions of dollars in new program funds that require quick distribution and keen oversight.

Recent HUD OIG Work

Office of Audit

A Mortgage Underwriting Review of 15 FHA Lenders Demonstrated That HUD Missed Critical Opportunities to Recover Losses to the FHA Insurance Fund

In January 2010, the U.S. Department of Housing and Urban Development's (HUD) Office of Inspector General (OIG) began Operation Watchdog, an initiative to review the underwriting of 15 Federal Housing Administration (FHA) direct endorsement lenders having default and claim rates indicating lender performance problems. The FHA Commissioner had expressed concern regarding the increasing default and claim rates against the FHA insurance fund for failed loans, prompting this initiative.

Our review objective was to determine whether each lender underwrote its respective loans in accordance with FHA requirements. To accomplish the objective, we reviewed between 12 and 20 FHA loans underwritten by each of the 15 lenders that resulted in claims against the FHA insurance fund. We reported our results in individual memorandums to HUD. This summary memorandum compiles the results of the Operation Watchdog initiative and expresses OIG's concerns about systemic problems with the underwriting of FHA insured loans and the resulting costs to the FHA insurance fund for loans that should not have been insured.

We recommended in each of the 15 issued memorandums that HUD pursue appropriate remedies under the Program Fraud Civil Remedies Act against each lender and/or its principals for incorrectly certifying to the integrity of the data or that due diligence was exercised during the underwriting of the 140 questioned loans. These loans resulted in actual losses or were expected to result in losses to the FHA insurance fund of more than $11 million. Further, the lenders' improper certifications could result in affirmative civil enforcement actions of more than $23 million. We also recommended that HUD take appropriate administrative action against each lender and/or its principals.

Based on the overall results of the Operation Watchdog initiative and the systemic problems identified, we made an additional recommendation to HUD that it develop and implement procedures to review a statistical or risk-based selection of loans for which FHA paid a claim on the mortgage insurance within the first two years of endorsement, to verify that the loans met FHA requirements and were qualified for insurance. We further recommended that these procedures include a requirement for HUD to seek appropriate civil and administrative remedies to recover losses incurred on loans not qualified for FHA insurance.

Report 2011-CF-1801, March 2, 2011

Civil Enforcement Actions

HUD OIG, HUD's Enforcement Center, and the Department of Justice Civil Enforcement Division is working together to take civil action against the fifteen Operation Watch Dog lenders. As of March 31, 2011, one lender has agreed to a settlement, eight lenders are being actively worked for civil enforcement, and remaining six are out of business.

Office of Investigations

Paul Allen, the former chief executive officer of Taylor, Bean & Whitaker Mortgage Corporation (Taylor, Bean & Whitaker), a former Federal Housing Administration (FHA)-approved direct endorsement lender and Government National Mortgage Association (Ginnie Mae) issuer, pled guilty in U.S. District Court to making false statements and committing a conspiracy.

In addition, Lee Farkas, the former chairman of Taylor, Bean & Whitaker, was convicted of committing a conspiracy and bank, wire, and securities fraud. Between 2002 and 2009, Farkas, Allen, and other individuals conspired and provided false information, sold phony and previously pledged loans to investors in the secondary mortgage market, and caused Taylor, Bean & Whitaker to submit false statements to the U.S. Department of Housing and Urban Development (HUD), Ginnie Mae, and other financial entities.

HUD, Ginnie Mae, and other financial entities realized losses in excess of $1.9 billion. The HUD Office of Inspector General (OIG), the Federal Bureau of Investigation (FBI), the Special IG for the Troubled Asset Relief Program, the Federal Deposit Insurance Corporation OIG, and the Federal Housing Finance Agency OIG conducted this investigation.

Office of Inspector General
Department of the Treasury

The Department of the Treasury's Office of Inspector General (OIG) was established pursuant to the 1988 amendments to the Inspector General Act of 1978. The Treasury Inspector General is appointed by the President, with the advice and consent of the Senate. Treasury OIG performs independent, objective reviews of Treasury programs and operations, except for those of the Internal Revenue Service (IRS) and the Troubled Asset Relief Program (TARP), and keeps the Secretary of the Treasury and Congress fully informed.[14] Treasury OIG is comprised of five divisions: (1) Office of Audit, (2) Office of Investigations, (3) Office of Small Business Lending Fund Program Oversight, (4) Office of Counsel, and (5) Office of Management. Treasury OIG is headquartered in Washington, DC, and has an audit office in Boston, MA.

The Treasury OIG has oversight responsibility for two federal banking agencies--the Office of the Comptroller of the Currency (OCC) and the Office of Thrift Supervision (OTS).[15] Together, these two agencies are responsible for 1,487 national banks and 731 thrifts with total assets of $9.4 trillion, comprising 79 percent of the U.S. banking system. The Treasury OIG also oversees several new offices and functions created by the Dodd-Frank Act such as the Office of Financial Research and Federal Insurance Office. The Treasury OIG has joint oversight with the Board of Governors of the Federal Reserve System OIG of the Bureau of Consumer Financial Protection (CFPB), also created by Dodd-Frank, until a CFPB Director of the bureau is confirmed by the Senate. That is because the Secretary of the Treasury is authorized to perform most, but not all, CFPB functions until a director is confirmed.[16] Furthermore, the Treasury OIG oversees certain Treasury functions related to Fannie Mae and Freddie Mac under the Housing and Economic Recovery Act of 2008, to include Treasury's Preferred Stock Purchase Agreement Program for the purpose of maintaining a positive net worth for both entities ($47.5 billion for fiscal year 2011), and Treasury's Mortgage-Backed Securities Purchase Program which was intended to help stabilize the mortgage market ($94.5 billion held as of June 30, 2011). Finally, related to Treasury's role in the economic recovery, the Treasury OIG oversees approximately $24 billion in non-IRS Recovery Act funds.

By statute, the Treasury Inspector General also serves as the Chair of the Council of Inspectors General on Financial Oversight, and as a member of the Recovery Act Accountability and Transparency Board.

---

14   The Treasury Inspector General for Tax Administration performs oversight of IRS, and a Special Inspector General performs oversight of TARP.

15   Pursuant to the Dodd-Frank Act, the functions of OTS are scheduled to transfer to OCC, FDIC, and FRB on July 21, 2011, and OTS is to be abolished 90 days later. OTS functions are being transferred principally to OCC.

16   Among the CFPB functions that cannot be performed, by the Treasury Secretary or anyone else, until a director is confirmed, is the exercise of the bureau's authority to (1) prohibit unfair, deceptive, or abusive acts or practices in connection with consumer financial products and services;(2) prescribe rules and require model disclosure forms to ensure that the features of a consumer financial product or service are fairly, accurately, and effectively disclosed; and (3) supervise rulemaking functions over non-depository institutions.

Failed Bank Reviews

In 1991, Congress enacted the Federal Deposit Insurance Corporation Improvement Act (FDICIA) amending the Federal Deposit Insurance Act (FDIA) following the failures of about a thousand banks and thrifts from 1986 to 1990. The amendments require that banking regulators take specified supervisory actions when they identify unsafe or unsound practices or conditions. Also added was a requirement that the Inspector General for the primary federal regulator of a failed financial institution conduct a material loss review when the estimated loss to the Deposit Insurance Fund is "material." As part of the MLR, OIG auditors determine the causes of the failure and assess the supervision of the institution, including the implementation of the prompt corrective action provisions of the act.[17] As appropriate, the Treasury OIG also makes recommendations for preventing any such loss in the future.

Prior to the enactment of the Dodd-Frank Act in July 2010, FDICIA defined a material loss as a loss to the Deposit Insurance Fund that exceeded the greater of $25 million or 2 percent of the institution's total assets. The Dodd-Frank Act redefined this threshold for triggering a material loss review to a loss that exceeds $200 million for 2010 and 2011, $150 million for 2012 and 2013, and $50 million for 2014 and thereafter (with a provision to temporarily raise the threshold to $75 million in certain circumstances). The act also requires a review of all bank failures with losses under these threshold amounts for the purposes of (1) ascertaining the grounds identified by the federal banking agency for appointing the Federal Deposit Insurance Corporation (FDIC) as receiver and (2) determining whether any unusual circumstances exist that might warrant a more in-depth review of the loss. This provision applies to bank failures from October 1, 2009, forward.

From the beginning of the current economic crisis in 2007 through June 30, 2011, the federal banking agencies have closed 372 banks and thrifts. One hundred and seven (107) of these were Treasury-regulated financial institutions. Of these 107 failures, 54 resulted in a material loss to the Deposit Insurance, so an MLR was required. As of June 30, 2011, we completed 26 MLRs—13 of OCC-regulated failed institutions and 13 of OTS-regulated failed institutions. In total, the estimated loss to the Deposit Insurance Fund for these 26 failures was $23.4 billion. We also completed a joint evaluation with the FDIC OIG of the failed Washington Mutual Bank (WaMu); although WaMu did not result in a loss to the Deposit Insurance Fund, it was the largest bank failure in U.S. history. Some of our overarching observations from this and other reviews performed by Treasury OIG are summarized below. As of the end of the reporting period, we had 28 MLRs in progress with estimated losses to the Deposit Insurance Fund totaling $10.4 billion.

From the evaluation of the WaMu failure and the 26 completed MLRs, we have seen a number of trends emerge. With respect to the causes of institutions' failures, we found poor underwriting and overly aggressive growth strategies fueled by volatile and costly wholesale funding (e.g., brokered deposits, Federal Home Loan Bank loans); risky lending products such as option adjustable rate mortages (option ARMs); high asset concentrations to include commercial real estate loans; and inadequate risk management systems. In addition, the management and boards of these institutions were often not effective in recognizing,

---

17   Prompt corrective action is a framework of supervisory actions for insured institutions that are not adequately capitalized. It was intended to ensure that action is taken when an institution becomes financially troubled in order to prevent a failure or minimize the resulting losses. These actions become increasingly severe as the institution falls into lower capital categories. The capital categories are well-capitalized, adequately capitalized, undercapitalized, significantly undercapitalized, and critically undercapitalized.

monitoring, or managing their risks. The economic recession and the decline in the real estate market were also contributing factors in most of the failures.

With respect to OCC's and OTS's supervision, we found that the regulators conducted regular and timely examinations and identified operational problems, but were slow to take timely and aggressive enforcement action. We also found that in rating these institutions, examiners gave too much weight to the fact that the institutions were profitable and their loans were performing and not enough weight given to the amount of risk that these institutions had taken on. We also noted that regulators took the appropriate prompt corrective action actions when warranted but those actions did not save the institutions. While it is too soon to comment on the general effectiveness of the prompt corrective action provisions of FDICIA, this is an area we and the OIGs of FDIC and FRB are joint examining and plan to report on later in the fiscal year.

Following is a discussion of two failed bank reviews that are illustrative of the general trends we have reported.

Federal Regulatory Oversight of Washington Mutual Bank of Seattle, Washington (closed September 25, 2008; estimated loss to the Deposit Insurance Fund – none at this time)

As mentioned above, we conducted a joint evaluation with the FDIC OIG of the failure of WaMu, the largest bank failure in U.S. history. On September 25, 2008, OTS, the thrift's primary federal regulator, closed WaMu and appointed FDIs review was not statutorily required. However, given WaMu's size, the circumstances leading up to WaMu's sale, and other losses (e.g., shareholder equity), the Treasury Inspector General and the FDIC Inspector General believed that a review was warranted.

We reported that WaMu failed primarily because of management's pursuit of a high-risk lending strategy that included liberal underwriting standards and inadequate risk controls. WaMu's high-risk strategy, combined with the housing and mortgage market collapse in mid-2007, left WaMu with loan losses, borrowing capacity limitations, and a falling stock price. In September 2008, depositors withdrew significant funds after high-profile failures of other financial institutions and rumors of WaMu's problems. WaMu was unable to raise capital to keep pace with depositor withdrawals, prompting OTS to close the institution.

OTS's examinations of WaMu identified concerns with WaMu's high-risk lending strategy, including repeat findings concerning WaMu's single family loan underwriting, management weaknesses, and inadequate internal controls. However, OTS's supervision did not ensure that WaMu corrected those problems early enough to prevent a failure of the institution. Furthermore, OTS largely relied on a WaMu system to track the thrift's progress in implementing corrective actions on hundreds of OTS examination findings.

We made a number of recommendations to OTS as a result of completed MLRs of failed thrifts during the current economic crisis. These recommendations applied to WaMu as well. They pertain to taking more timely formal enforcement action when circumstances warrant, ensuring that CAMELS[18] ratings are properly supported, reminding examiners of the risks associated with rapid growth and high-risk concentrations, ensuring thrifts have sound internal risk management systems, ensuring repeat conditions are reviewed and corrected, and requiring thrifts to hold adequate capital. OTS has taken or plans to take action in response to

---

18   CAMELS is an acronym for performance rating components for financial institutions: Capital adequacy, Asset quality, Management administration, Earnings, Liquidity, and Sensitivity to market risk. Numerical values range from 1 to 5, with 1 being the best rating and 5 being the worst. Each institution is also assigned a composite rating based on an assessment of its overall condition and level of supervisory concern.

these recommendations. Additionally, OTS established a large bank unit to oversee regional supervision of institutions with assets of more than $10 billion. In the WaMu report, we also specifically recommended that OTS use its own system to track the status of recommendations and related corrective actions. OTS concurred with our recommendation and has completed action to address it.

Our joint report also made several observations about FDIC's role as the deposit insurer for WaMu and included two recommendations to the FDIC Chairman. (EVAL-10-002)

On April 16, 2010, the Treasury Inspector General and the FDIC Inspector General testified about the results of the joint evaluation of WaMu before the Permanent Subcommittee on Investigations of the Senate Committee on Homeland Security and Governmental Affairs. The testimony was part of the subcommittee's hearing entitled Wall Street and the Financial Crisis: The Role of Bank Regulators. (OIG-CA-10-006)

Material Loss Review of IndyMac Bank of Pasadena, California (closed July 11, 2008; estimated loss to the Deposit Insurance Fund - $10.7 billion)

We reported that IndyMac's failure was largely related to its business strategy of originating and securitizing Alt-A loans on a large scale. This strategy resulted in rapid growth and a high concentration of risky assets. IndyMac's aggressive growth strategy, use of Alt-A and other nontraditional loan products, insufficient underwriting, credit concentrations in residential real estate in the California and Florida markets, and heavy reliance on costly funds borrowed from the Federal Home Loan Bank and from brokered deposits, led to its demise when the mortgage market declined in 2007. IndyMac often made loans without verification of the borrower's income or assets, and to borrowers with poor credit histories. Appraisals on underlying collateral were often questionable as well. IndyMac's business model was to offer loan products to fit the borrower's needs, using an extensive array of risky option ARMs, subprime loans, 80/20 loans, and other nontraditional products. Ultimately, loans were made to many borrowers who simply could not afford them. When home prices declined in the latter half of 2007 and the secondary mortgage market collapsed, IndyMac was forced to hold $10.7 billion of loans it could not sell in the secondary market. Its reduced liquidity was further exacerbated in late June 2008 when account holders withdrew $1.55 billion in deposits. This "run" on the thrift followed the public release of a letter from Senator Charles Schumer to FDIC and OTS. The letter outlined the Senator's concerns with IndyMac. While the run was a contributing factor in the timing of IndyMac's demise, the underlying cause of the failure was the unsafe and unsound manner in which the thrift was operated.

Although OTS conducted timely and regular examinations of IndyMac and provided oversight through off-site monitoring, its supervision of the thrift failed to prevent a material loss to the Deposit Insurance Fund. The thrift's high-risk business strategy warranted more careful and much earlier attention. That said, OTS did identify numerous problems and risks, including the quantity and poor quality of nontraditional mortgage products, but did not take aggressive action to stop those practices from continuing to proliferate. OTS relied on the cooperation of IndyMac management to make needed improvements. However, IndyMac had a long history of not fully addressing OTS findings. From 2001 to 2007, OTS's CAMELS ratings of IndyMac consistently remained at 2. It was not until 2008 that OTS dropped IndyMac's rating to a 3 and then to a 5. OTS did not issue any enforcement action, either informal or formal, until June 2008. In short, earlier enforcement action was warranted.

Our report pointed to the need for OTS senior leadership to reflect carefully on the supervision that was exercised over IndyMac and ensure that the correct lessons were taken away from its failure. Among other things, we recommended that OTS caution its examiners that assigning composite CAMELS ratings of 1 or 2 to thrifts with high-risk, aggressive growth strategies need to be supported with compelling, verified mitigating factors (such as thrift corporate governance, and risk management and underwriting controls) that are likely to be sustainable. OTS management agreed with our overall findings and recommendations. As mentioned in our discussion of WaMu above, among the actions planned by OTS was the establishment of a large savings association unit in Washington, DC, to review regional office actions for savings associations with total assets above $10 billion. We noted that while the planned actions were positive, it will take time to assess their effectiveness and continuous senior management attention will be crucial to their success. (OIG-09-032)

While the reviews highlighted above involved failed institutions regulated by OTS, our material loss reviews of OCC-regulated failed institutions have identified similar problems.

Consumer Financial Protection Bureau Oversight

On January 10, 2011, the OIGs of Treasury and the Board of Governors of the Federal Reserve System (FRB) jointly issued a letter that responded to a November 22, 2010, congressional request for information related to CFPB's transparency, organizational structure, and regulatory agenda. In order to respond, we (1) reviewed the applicable sections of the Dodd-Frank Act and other relevant laws, (2) requested, obtained, and reviewed relevant information and documentation from the FRB and Treasury, and (3) interviewed key Treasury officials, including Professor Elizabeth Warren who is serving as the Special Assistant to the President and Special Advisor to the Secretary of the Treasury on CFPB.

As noted in our letter, the Treasury Secretary delegated his interim authority to establish CFPB to Professor Warren and other Treasury officials. According to Treasury, Professor Warren's implementation activities are overseen by the Secretary, and she has regular meetings with senior Treasury officials regarding the status of start-up efforts and the priorities she has identified for CFPB.

Our response noted that Treasury implemented a policy to disclose meetings regarding CFPB-related activities between senior Treasury officials, including Professor Warren, and individuals from private sector entities. In addition, Treasury noted that Professor Warren's schedule had been, and would continue to be, posted on its website.

With respect to organizational structure, we responded that CFPB had prepared a draft organizational plan and we identified, as requested, the names of Treasury and FRB employees and detailees in certain specified categories of positions, such as members of the Senior Executive Service, who were working to build the Bureau's infrastructure. We also reported that to support implementation activities, CFPB requested and received from FRB nearly $33 million. With regard to the regulatory agenda, Professor Warren provided examples of two policy initiatives that will receive priority: (1) consolidating duplicative and overlapping mortgage disclosure forms mandated by the Truth in Lending Act and the Real Estate Settlement Procedures Act and (2) simplifying credit card agreements to ensure that customers fully understand fees and finance charges.

Finally, our response advised that Treasury's interim authority extends beyond the designated transfer date if CFPB does not have its Director in place at that time. After the July 21, 2011, designated transfer date and until a Director is confirmed by the Senate, the Treasury Secretary has the authority to carry out certain CFPB functions, which include prescribing rules, conducting examinations, and enforcing orders. Treasury cannot, however, exercise certain of CFPB newly established authorities, which include prohibiting unfair, deceptive, or abusive acts or practices. (OIG-CA-11-004)

As noted above, Treasury OIG currently shares joint oversight responsibility for CFPB with FRB OIG. As part of this joint oversight responsibility, our offices initiated a review to assess CFPB's development and execution of an implementation plan and timeline to establish the bureau's functions. The objectives are to evaluate CFPB's efforts to (1) identify mission-critical activities and legislative mandates, (2) develop and execute a comprehensive implementation plan and timeline for mission-critical activities and legislative mandates, and (3) communicate its implementation plan and timeline to key stakeholder. This work is currently ongoing.

Congressional Request for Information Regarding Economic Analysis by OCC

In a May 4, 2011 letter, the Ranking Member and other members of the U.S. Senate Committee on Banking, Housing, and Urban Affairs expressed concern that regulatory agencies are conducting rulemakings to implement specific provisions of the Dodd-Frank Act without adequately considering the costs and benefits of their rules and the effects those rules could have on the economy. The letter requested that Treasury OIG initiate and report on a review of the economic analyses performed by OCC for three proposed rules: (1) *Credit Risk Retention*, (2) *Margin and Capital Requirements for Covered Swap Entities*, and (3) *Risk-Based Capital Standards: Advanced Capital Adequacy Framework – Basel II; Establishment of a Risk-Based Capital Floor*.[19]

We found that OCC has processes in place to ensure that required economic analyses are performed consistently and with rigor in connection with its rulemaking authority. We found that those processes were followed for the three proposed rules we reviewed. Specifically, we determined that OCC used quantitative and qualitative methodologies; considered alternatives and the impact of the alternatives; sought public input; and that OCC rulemaking was transparent and the results were generally reproducible. We did identify the need for OCC to (1) develop procedures to ensure coordination between the OCC groups calculating administrative burden for various analyses and (2) update internal guidance to reflect the current statutory environment governing the rulemaking and related economic analysis processes. OCC agreed with our recommendations. Additionally, we noted in our report that there was no formal process in place that provides for coordination on economic analyses between OCC and the other federal banking agencies. (OIG-CA-11-006)

---

19   Similar requests were made to the Inspectors General of FDIC, Board of Governors of the Federal Reserve System, Commodity Futures Trading Commission, and Securities and Exchange Commission for reviews of economic analyses performed in connection with rulemaking by their respective agencies.

Review of Plan for Transfer of OTS Personnel and Functions to the OCC, FDIC, and FRB

In collaboration with the OIGs of FDIC and FRB, we reviewed the Joint Implementation Plan (Plan) prepared by the FRB, FDIC, OCC, and OTS. The Plan details the steps the agencies will take to implement the provisions of Title III, *Transfer of Powers to the Comptroller of the Currency, the Corporation, and the Board of Governors*, of the Dodd-Frank Act. Section 327 of Title III mandated the preparation of the Plan and our offices' review.

We reported that the Plan generally conforms to the provisions of sections 301 through 326 of Title III. However, we did note an omission in the Plan in that it did not address the prohibition against involuntary separation or relocation of transferred OTS employees for 30 months (except under certain circumstances). We recommended that the Plan be amended to address this requirement. We also reported that, while not impacting our overall conclusion on the Plan, certain details need to be worked out to ensure that OTS employees are not unfairly disadvantaged and an orderly transfer of OTS powers, authority, and employees can be effectively accomplished. Finally, we reported on several other matters associated with the transfer of OTS functions, including an OTS pension fund, savings association assessments, and financial reporting by OTS. (OIG-11-064)

We will monitor these issues and implementation of the Plan, and report on the progress to transfer the OTS functions every 6 months, as required by the Act.

In-Progress Joint Review of Prompt Regulatory Action

We are conducting a review of the Prompt Regulatory Action (PRA) provisions of the FDIA in collaboration with the FDIC and FRB OIGs. The PRA provisions of the FDIA, enacted as part of FDICIA, include section 38 (Prompt Corrective Action (PCA)) and section 39 (Standards for Safety and Soundness). Sections 38 and 39 were intended to assist in the identification of problem banks and provide tools for regulators to ensure consistent, timely enforcement action designed to minimize losses to the Deposit Insurance Fund.

This work will determine the purpose of and circumstances that led to the PRA provisions and the lessons learned from the savings and loan crisis in the 1980s and early 1990s; evaluate to what extent PCA and the Standards for Safety and Soundness were a factor in bank failures and problem banks during the current crisis; assess whether the PRA provisions prompted federal regulators to act more quickly and more forcefully to limit losses to the Deposit Insurance Fund; and determine whether there are other non-capital measures that provide a leading indication of risks to the insurance fund that should be considered as part of the PRA provisions.

Treasury Management and Performance Challenges Related to Financial Regulation and Economic Recovery

In accordance with the Reports Consolidation Act of 2000, the Treasury Inspector General annually provides the Treasury Secretary with his perspective on the most serious management and performance challenges facing the Department. In a memorandum to Secretary Geithner dated October 22, 2010, Inspector General Thorson reported two management and performance challenges that were specifically directed towards financial regulation and economic recovery. Those challenges were: Transformation of Financial Regulation and Management of Treasury's Authorities Intended to Support and Improve the Economy.

Transformation of Financial Regulation

With the intention to prevent, or at least minimize, the impact of a future financial sector crisis on the U.S. economy, the Dodd-Frank Act placed a great deal of responsibility within Treasury and on the Treasury Secretary. Accordingly, this challenge, among other things, primarily focused on a number of Dodd-Frank Act mandates related to Treasury. It broadly addressed the challenge of implementing an effective Financial Stability Oversight Council (FSOC) that timely identifies and strongly responds to emerging risks. It included Treasury's role in standing up CFPB. It addressed two new mandated offices to be established within Treasury: the Office of Financial Research and the Federal Insurance Office. It discussed the act's effort to streamline the supervision of depository institutions and holding companies by requiring the transfer the powers and duties of OTS to OCC, FRB, and FDIC.

This management and performance challenge also included the other regulatory challenges that the Treasury Inspector General had previously reported. Specifically, it acknowledged the number of Treasury-regulated financial institutions that failed since the beginning of the current economic crisis and their multi-billion losses to the Deposit Insurance Fund. With respect to those failures and associated losses, the challenge stated that although many factors contributed to the turmoil in the financial markets, our work found that OCC and OTS did not identify early or force timely correction of unsafe and unsound practices by numerous institutions under their supervision. Among other things, we also spoke to the irresponsible lending practices of many institutions, including reliance on risky products, such as option ARMs, and degradation of underwriting standards as well as high asset concentrations in commercial real estate and overreliance on unpredictable brokered deposits.

Management of Treasury's Authorities Intended to Support and Improve the Economy

This challenge, among other things, focused on a number of broad authorities the Congress provided to Treasury to address the financial crisis under the Housing and Economic Recovery Act and the Emergency Economic Stabilization Act, both enacted in 2008, the American Recovery and Reinvestment Act of 2009 (Recovery Act), and the Small Business Jobs Act of 2010. It acknowledged that certain authorities in the Housing and Economic Recovery Act and the Emergency Economic Stabilization Act expired, but pointed out the fact that challenges remain in managing Treasury's outstanding investments. In contrast, program administration for the Recovery Act is still evolving, and the Small Business Jobs Act programs must be stood up.

As a final note, another challenge that the Treasury Inspector General reported for a number of years is Treasury's anti-money laundering and terrorist financing/Bank Secrecy Act enforcement efforts. Among other things, this challenge pointed out our particular concern with respect to the current economic environment. Specifically, we expressed our concern that financial institutions and their regulators may have decreased their attention to Bank Secrecy Act and foreign sanctions program compliance as they address safety and soundness concerns during the current economic crisis.

Office of Inspector General
The Federal Deposit Insurance Corporation

The Federal Deposit Insurance Corporation (FDIC) was created by the Congress in 1933 as an independent agency to maintain stability and public confidence in the nation's banking system by insuring deposits and independently regulating state-chartered, non-member banks. The Deposit Insurance Fund (DIF) protects depositors from losses due to failures of insured commercial banks and thrifts. According to March 2011 data, the FDIC insured approximately $6.4 trillion in deposits at 7,574 banks and savings associations, and promoted the safety and soundness of these institutions by identifying, monitoring, and addressing risks to which they are exposed. The FDIC was the primary federal regulator for 4,664, or over 61 percent of the insured institutions.

The FDIC Office of Inspector General (OIG) is an independent and objective unit established under the Inspector General Act of 1978, as amended. Our mission is to promote the economy, efficiency, and effectiveness of FDIC programs and operations, and protect against fraud, waste, and abuse. In doing so, we can assist and augment the FDIC's contribution to stability and public confidence in the nation's financial system. We have undertaken a comprehensive body of work during the past 2½ years of the financial crisis to carry out that mission.

The FDIC OIG's audit work over this time frame has focused principally on mandatory reviews of failed FDIC-supervised institutions. We have issued a total of 185 products (material loss reviews (MLR), in-depth reviews, and failed bank reviews) over the past 30 months. This work has made an impact on FDIC supervision that will last for years to come. As a follow-on to this work, we also examined the actions that the FDIC has taken in response to our failed bank work in a capstone report addressing the FDIC's supervisory enhancements over the past several years.

Investigative work at both open and closed banks complements the reviews of failed banks. This work provides additional insights into the causes for institution failures and the control weaknesses that allow perpetrators of fraud to commit illegal acts undermining the integrity of the financial services industry.

In a related vein, we have also reviewed matters related to the failures of two important institutions for which the FDIC was not the primary federal regulator—IndyMac Bank and Washington Mutual Bank. In both cases, our work focused on the FDIC's unique role as insurer and back-up regulator for these institutions.

In response to a requirement of the Dodd-Frank Wall Street Reform and Consumer Protection Act (Dodd-Frank Act), we also conducted a review with the Department of the Treasury and Federal Reserve OIGs addressing the transfer of Office of Thrift Supervision (OTS) functions to the FDIC, Office of the Comptroller of the Currency (OCC), and Federal Reserve. Additionally, in connection with the Dodd-Frank Act, at the request of 10 minority members (Members) of the U.S. Senate Committee on Banking, Housing, and Urban Affairs, we undertook a review of the FDIC's rulemaking efforts for three specific rules, with particular attention to the cost-benefit analyses that the FDIC undertakes regarding such rulemaking.

Finally, we are conducting a review stemming from our failed bank work that is focusing on two prompt regulatory action-related sections in the Federal Deposit Insurance Act mandating that regulators establish a two-part regulatory framework for improving safeguards for the DIF. One focuses on capital levels and the second focuses on other measures of an institution's safety and soundness. That effort is ongoing and we are coordinating with the Treasury and Federal Reserve OIGs in conducting this work.

All of these efforts are discussed in more detail below.

Failed Bank Work Identifies Trends Contributing to FDIC-Supervised Institution Failures

In May 2009, quite early-on in our MLR work, the OIG identified and shared with the FDIC Audit Committee and FDIC management our perspectives on MLR trends based on six completed and two draft MLR reports.

Based on that early work, we suggested that greater consideration of risk in assigning CAMELS[20] ratings appeared to be needed. Risky behaviors that did not seem to have had a meaningful impact on CAMELS ratings included: pursuit of aggressive growth in commercial real estate and acquisition, development, and construction loans; excessive levels of asset concentration with little risk mitigation; reliance on wholesale funding to fund asset growth; ineffective leadership from bank boards of directors and management; inadequate loan underwriting and lack of other loan portfolio and risk management controls, including appropriate use of interest reserves; allowance for loan and lease losses methodology and funding; and compensation arrangements that were tied to quantity of loans rather than quality.

We also identified special issues with regard to "de novo" or newly chartered institutions, and we emphasized the need to monitor business plans closely; consider growth exceeding the plan as a risk to be managed; and ensure that management expertise and operations/administrative structures kept pace with asset growth. We further observed that Prompt Corrective Action (PCA) did not appear to have prevented failure of the institutions we had reviewed to date. Also, examiners generally had not used the non-capital provisions of PCA to curtail activities that contributed to losses to the DIF.

Our MLR work over the ensuing months continued to validate the earlier issues we identified, and other issues contributing to institution failures and losses surfaced in subsequent reviews. These included, for example, banks that had purchased loan participations—sometimes out-of-territory— in order to rapidly grow the loan portfolio or as a change in strategic business direction. In some cases, the banks did not conduct adequate due diligence or adequately administer these loans after purchase. We saw instances of significant losses related to collateralized debt obligations, collateralized mortgage obligations, and government-sponsored enterprise stocks such as the Federal National Mortgage Association (Fannie Mae) and the Federal Home Loan Mortgage Corporation (Freddie Mac) preferred stock. In some cases as well, banks had

---

20   Financial institution regulators use the Uniform Financial Institutions Rating System to evaluate a bank's performance in the six components represented by the **CAMELS** acronym: **C**apital Adequacy, **A**sset Quality, **M**anagement, **E**arnings, **L**iquidity, and **S**ensitivity to Market Risk. Each component, and an overall composite score, is assigned a rating of 1 through 5, with 1 having the least regulatory concern and 5 having the greatest concern.

concentrations in large borrowing relationships and may not have properly assessed the borrower's global financial condition, including the impact that problems on projects financed at other institutions might have on the borrower's repayment capacity. With respect to bank Boards and management, we noted in some of our MLRs instances where there was a lack of sufficient expertise or an inability to deal with a sudden change in business strategy, for example purchasing complex credit products without knowledgeable staff on board to handle these products. Although often identified through the FDIC's on-site examination process or off-site monitoring tools, such risky practices were not always acted upon early enough for corrective action to be effective.

FDIC Makes Enhancements to Its Supervisory Activities

Based on the OIG's body of MLR work, we found it important to conduct a review to determine how the FDIC's supervision program had changed to address issues identified related to the failures of the past few years and any emerging issues. At the time of our fieldwork, which was as of August 20, 2010, 118 additional FDIC-insured financial institutions had failed since issuance of our May 2009 memorandum. In addition, as of the same period, we had issued 57 more MLR reports on 64 failures of FDIC-supervised institutions.

We reviewed the broader inventory of failures and reported in our follow-on review that the FDIC had taken a number of positive steps to enhance its supervision program. Of particular note, the FDIC:

- emphasized a forward-looking supervisory approach, which is embodied in a comprehensive training program and various financial institution and examiner guidance, including guidance related to de novo banks;

- implemented other cross-cutting initiatives such as establishing relevant Corporate Performance Goals in 2009 and 2010 specifically related to some MLR issues;

- implemented a post-MLR assessment process to identify lessons learned from the bank failures and conclusions included in our MLR final reports and solicit input from its examination staff regarding suggested changes to policies and procedures. This process also resulted in the identification of potential best practices related to the FDIC's examinations;

- enhanced offsite monitoring activities;

- enhanced coordination between its risk management and compliance examination functions;

- improved interagency coordination for charter conversions;

- worked with the other federal regulatory agencies to implement a new agreement associated with the FDIC's backup examination authority; and

- engaged in interagency efforts to address some of the more systemic MLR trends, such as capital definitions and levels, and liquidity.

We made recommendations, with which management concurred, intended to further improve the FDIC's supervision program. These related to updating or reviewing guidance regarding, for example, commercial real estate and acquisition, development and construction lending; concentrations; de novo bank supervision; dominant bank officials; large borrower relationships; and participation loans.

OIG Investigations Target Financial Institution Fraud

Investigative work at both open and closed banks complements the audits and evaluations we have conducted and provides additional insights into the causes for institution failures and the control weaknesses that allow perpetrators of fraud to pursue illegal acts undermining the integrity of the financial services industry. Our office is committed to partnerships with other OIGs, the Department of Justice (DOJ), the Federal Bureau of Investigation (FBI), and other state and local law enforcement agencies in pursuing such criminal acts and helping to deter fraud, waste, and abuse.

Our current caseload includes 223 active investigations. Of these, 114 relate to open bank matters and 109 to closed bank matters. These cases involve fraud and other misconduct on the part of senior bank officials, and include mortgage and commercial loan fraud exposed by turmoil in the housing, commercial real estate, and lending industries. The perpetrators of such crimes can be those very individuals entrusted with governance responsibilities at the institutions—directors and bank officers. In other cases, individuals providing professional services to the banks and customers, others working inside the bank, and customers themselves are principals in fraudulent schemes. Other investigations include cases involving concealment of assets, misrepresentations of FDIC insurance or affiliation, and computer crimes. The OIG's success in all such investigations contributes to ensuring the continued safety and soundness of the nation's banks.

FDIC OIG investigative results over the past 2½-year period include the following: 370 indictments; 226 arrests; 268 convictions, and fines, restitution, and other monetary recoveries of more than $597.4 million.

One recent case to which our office devoted substantial resources deserves special mention as one of the largest bank frauds in history. The former chairman and owner of Taylor, Bean & Whitaker (TBW) was sentenced on June 30, 2011 to 30 years in prison and ordered to forfeit approximately $38.5 million for his role in a more than $2.9 billion fraud scheme that contributed to the failure of TBW and Colonial Bank. At one time, TBW was one of the largest privately held mortgage lending companies in the United States and Colonial Bank was one of the 25 largest banks in the United States. The failure of Colonial Bank caused a $4.2 billion loss to the DIF.

Six other individuals pleaded guilty earlier and received stiff sentences for their roles in the fraud scheme. A former senior vice president of Colonial Bank and head of the Mortgage Warehouse Lending Division was sentenced to 8 years in prison. The former treasurer of TBW was sentenced to 6 years in prison. TBW's former chief executive officer was sentenced to 40 months in prison. The former president of TBW was sentenced to 30 months in prison. A former operations supervisor for Colonial Bank's Mortgage Warehouse Lending Division and a former senior financial analyst at TBW were each sentenced to 3 months in prison.

The successful outcomes of this case reflect the coordinated efforts of the DOJ, the FBI, U.S Attorney's Office for the Eastern District of Virginia, FDIC OIG, Special Inspector General for the Troubled Asset Relief Program, Housing and Urban Development OIG, and Federal Housing Finance Agency OIG. The Internal Revenue Service Criminal Investigation Division, Securities and Exchange Commission, and Financial Crimes Enforcement Network of the Department of the Treasury also assisted.

OIG Reviews of IndyMac Bank and Washington Mutual Bank Provide Insights to the FDIC's Unique Role as Insurer and Back-up Regulator

The FDIC is the primary federal regulator (PFR) for state non-member banks, but has the unique role of insuring deposits for all depository institutions in the United States. In its capacity as insurer, the FDIC is responsible for regularly monitoring and assessing the potential risks at all insured institutions, including those for which it is not the PFR. Additionally, the FDIC, by statute, has special examination authority and certain enforcement authority for all insured depository institutions for which it is not the PFR. Two key assignments over the past several years have highlighted important points related to the FDIC's unique role as insurer.

IndyMac Bank: OTS closed IndyMac Federal Savings Bank (IndyMac) on July 11, 2008. As of July 31, 2009, the estimated cost of the resolution to the DIF was approximately $10.7 billion. The OTS was the PFR for IndyMac and was statutorily responsible for conducting full-scope on-site examinations of the bank to assess safety and soundness, and compliance with consumer protection laws and regulations. We conducted a review to evaluate the FDIC's back-up role in monitoring IndyMac.

We reported that in its role as insurer, the FDIC identified and monitored risks that IndyMac presented to the DIF by participating with the OTS in on-site examinations of the bank in 2001, 2002, 2003, and again shortly before IndyMac failed in 2008 and through the completion of required reports and analysis of the bank based upon information from FDIC monitoring systems. FDIC risk committees also raised broad concerns about the impact that an economic slowdown could have on institutions like IndyMac that were heavily involved in securitizations and subprime lending.

Nevertheless, FDIC officials consistently concluded that despite its high-risk profile, the bank posed an ordinary or slightly more than ordinary level of risk to the insurance fund. It was not until August 2007 that the FDIC began to understand the implications that the historic collapse of the credit market and housing slowdown could have on the bank and took additional actions to evaluate IndyMac Bank's viability.

We identified four matters for further study and consideration related to:

- Increased flexibility and independence in the FDIC's frameworks for establishing a supervisory approach and making deposit insurance determinations.

- Delegations of authority and reporting requirements surrounding back-up examination authority decisions.

- Appointment and transition of case managers for large, high-risk institutions.

- Authorities related to requesting back-up examinations and pursuing enforcement actions against non-supervised institutions.

Management's response to our report addressed steps underway to track all back-up examinations and to address case manager appointment and transition.

Washington Mutual Bank (WaMu): In a similar vein, about 9 months later, we conducted a joint review with the Department of the Treasury OIG related to the failure of WaMu on September 25, 2008. We issued our report on April 9, 2010. The work on WaMu supported and expanded upon concerns that we identified earlier with respect to IndyMac Bank.

WaMu was the largest bank failure in the history of the United States, but because the resolution structure resulted in no loss to the DIF, the threshold for conducting a material loss review was not triggered. However, it is estimated that WaMu's failure could have caused a loss of $41.5 billion to the DIF. Given the size, the circumstances leading up to the resolution, and the non-DIF losses (i.e., loss of shareholder value), we initiated a review with the Department of the Treasury OIG to determine the events leading to the need for the FDIC-facilitated transaction.

The team evaluated the OTS's supervision of WaMu, including implementation of PCA provisions of section 38, and the FDIC's supervision and monitoring of WaMu in its role as backup regulator and insurer. This evaluation was the first to comprehensively analyze the supervisory efforts of the OTS and the FDIC with respect to a single failure. The Department of the Treasury OIG focused on the causes of WaMu's failure and the OTS's supervision of the institution (discussed in the Treasury OIG section of this report). The FDIC OIG evaluated the FDIC's role as insurer and back-up supervisor.

At the time of its failure, WaMu was one of the eight largest federally insured financial institutions, operating 2,300 branches in 15 states, with total assets of $307 billion. WaMu was immediately merged with JP Morgan Chase & Co. and subsequently operated as part of JP Morgan Chase Bank, National Association, in Columbus, Ohio.

As for the FDIC's role, as the deposit insurer for WaMu, the FDIC was responsible for monitoring and assessing WaMu's risk to the DIF. As insurer, the FDIC had authority to perform its own back-up examination of WaMu and impose enforcement actions to protect the DIF, provided statutory and regulatory procedures were followed. The FDIC conducted its required monitoring of WaMu from 2003 to 2008 and identified risks with WaMu's lending strategy and internal controls. The risks noted in FDIC monitoring reports were not, however, reflected in WaMu's deposit insurance premium payments.

Based on our work, we identified two major concerns related to deposit insurance regulations and the interagency agreement governing the FDIC's back-up authority.

First, we concluded that the FDIC deposit insurance regulations were too restrictive in prescribing the information used to assign an institution's insurance category and premium rate. The team recommended that the FDIC Chairman, in consultation with the FDIC Board of Directors, revisit FDIC deposit insurance regulations to ensure those regulations provide the FDIC with the flexibility needed to make its own independent determination of an institution's risk to the DIF rather than relying too heavily on the PFR's risk examination results and on the institution's capital levels. We believed that the bank failures of this current economic crisis showed that factors other than examination ratings were better indicators of an institution's risk to the DIF.

Second, we concluded that the interagency agreement governing back-up examination did not provide the FDIC with the access to information that it needed to assess WaMu's risk to the DIF. As noted earlier, in the case of WaMu, if not for the FDIC-facilitated sale, WaMu's failure could have caused a $41.5 billion loss to the DIF. Although there is clearly a need to balance FDIC information needs and the regulatory burden imposed on a financial institution, we reported that the interagency agreement in place at the time did not allow the FDIC sufficient flexibility to obtain information necessary to assess risk in order to protect the DIF. As such, we recommended that the FDIC Chairman, in consultation with the FDIC Board of Directors, revisit the interagency agreement to ensure it provided the FDIC with sufficient access to the information necessary to assess an institution's risk to the DIF.

The joint efforts of the FDIC and Treasury OIGs produced an informative report that was well received by numerous stakeholders, including senior management of the OTS and the FDIC, and two testimonies presented to the Permanent Subcommittee on Investigations, Committee on Homeland Security and Governmental Affairs, U.S. Senate, by the Inspectors General of the Department of the Treasury and the FDIC. The report supported a number of earlier recommendations made by the Department of the Treasury OIG to enhance the OTS's supervision of the institutions it regulates and also made an additional recommendation, with which OTS agreed.

With respect to the FDIC, the report recommended changes to the level of access to information that the FDIC has to non-supervised institutions, and more significantly, changes to the types of business risks and factors that should be considered for pricing deposit insurance. The FDIC agreed with both recommendations and began implementing them immediately. Actions taken in connection with these recommendations and as a result of the Dodd-Frank Act have enhanced the FDIC's back-up authority and its conduct of special examinations, and brought about changes in its deposit insurance assessment system. The impact of this WaMu work has benefited the banking industry, the public, and the overall health of the DIF.

OIGs Review Plan for Transfer of OTS Personnel and Functions to the OCC, Federal Reserve, and FDIC

We joined our OIG colleagues at the Treasury and Federal Reserve OIGs to review a Joint Implementation Plan (Plan) prepared by the Federal Reserve Board (FRB), FDIC, OCC, and OTS. The Plan details the steps the agencies will take to implement the provisions of Title III, *Transfer of Powers to the Comptroller of the Currency, the Corporation, and the Board of Governors*, of the Dodd-Frank Act. Section 327 of Title III mandated the preparation of the Plan and our offices' review.

We conducted the review to determine whether the Plan conforms to the relevant provisions of the Dodd-Frank Act, to include determining whether the Plan (1) sufficiently takes into consideration the orderly transfer of personnel, (2) describes procedures and safeguards to ensure that OTS employees are not unfairly disadvantaged relative to employees of OCC and FDIC, (3) sufficiently takes into consideration the orderly transfer of authority and responsibilities, (4) sufficiently takes into consideration the effective transfer of funds, and (5) sufficiently takes into consideration the orderly transfer of property.

In brief, we concluded that the Plan generally conforms to the provisions of sections 301 through 326 of Title III. However, we did note an omission in the Plan in that it did not address the prohibition against involuntary separation or relocation of transferred OTS employees for 30 months (except under certain circumstances). We recommended that the Plan be amended to address this requirement.

We also found that, while not impacting our overall conclusion on the Plan, certain details need to be worked out to ensure that OTS employees are not unfairly disadvantaged and an orderly transfer of OTS powers, authority, and employees can be effectively accomplished. Finally, we reported on several other matters associated with the transfer of OTS functions, including an OTS pension fund, savings association assessments, and financial reporting by OTS.

We will monitor these issues and implementation of the Plan, and report on the progress to transfer the OTS functions every 6 months, as required by the Act.

OIG Conducts Dodd-Frank Rulemaking Assignment in Response to Congressional Request

By way of brief background, under the Dodd-Frank Act, the FDIC is required or authorized to implement some 44 regulations, including 18 independent and 26 joint rulemakings. Within the FDIC, each rulemaking effort is an interdivisional project that brings together personnel from FDIC Legal Division's Corporate, Consumer, Insurance and Legislation Branch; the Executive Secretary's Section; and the appropriate functional division such as the Division of Risk Management Supervision, Division of Resolutions and Receiverships, and the Division of Insurance and Research.

In a May 4, 2011 letter, 10 minority members (Members) of the U.S. Senate Committee on Banking, Housing, and Urban Affairs expressed concern that regulatory agencies are conducting rulemakings to implement specific provisions of the Dodd-Frank Act without adequately considering the costs and benefits of their rules and the effects those rules could have on the economy. The Members asked the Inspectors General from the FDIC, FRB, Commodity Futures Trading Commission, Department of the Treasury, and Securities and Exchange Commission to initiate a review of the economic analyses performed by their respective regulatory agency for specific rulemakings. In particular, the letter requested that our office prepare a report describing the economic analysis that the FDIC performed for three proposed rules: (1) *Credit Risk Retention*, (2) *Margin and Capital Requirements for Covered Swap Entities*, and (3) *Risk-Based Capital Standards: Advanced Capital Adequacy Framework – Basel II; Establishment of a Risk-Based Capital Floor.*

Additionally, the Members asked us to describe other rulemaking steps that would be required if the FDIC were subject to certain Executive Orders and Office of Management and Budget guidance. They also asked us to describe to what extent the FDIC is considering the cumulative burden of all Dodd-Frank Act rulemakings on market participants and the economy.

We found that the FDIC assigned highly qualified subject matter experts to develop the technical aspects of the proposed rules and to conduct economic analysis, where appropriate. We confirmed that these experts were knowledgeable of, and followed the applicable statutory and FDIC requirements related to, rulemaking and economic analysis. For each of the three rules, the FDIC worked jointly with other financial regulatory agencies; performed analysis of relevant data as required; considered alternative approaches to the extent allowed by the legislation; requested comments from the public; and, where appropriate, presented information supporting agency analysis and conclusions in the proposed rule. The FDIC is also considering the cumulative burden of all Dodd-Frank Act rulemakings and, among other things, has established a broad-based working group to evaluate the interrelationships of all Dodd-Frank rulemaking efforts.

Ongoing Work on the Role and Use of Prompt Regulatory Action Provisions

The Federal Deposit Insurance Corporation Improvement Act (FDICIA) of 1991 was enacted to make fundamental changes in federal oversight of depository institutions in response to the financial crisis of the 1980s and early 1990s. FDICIA's Prompt Regulatory Action provisions created two new sections in the Federal

Deposit Insurance (FDI) Act – sections 38 and 39 – which mandated that regulators establish a two-part regulatory framework for improving safeguards for the DIF. Section 38 focuses on capital levels and section 39 focuses on other measures of an institution's safety and soundness.

We are conducting a review in collaboration with the Department of the Treasury and Federal Reserve OIGs to further evaluate the role and federal regulators' use of the PRA provisions over the last several years in light of the significant increase in the number of troubled financial institutions and failures since mid-2007, a period when those provisions presumably would have come into play more frequently.

This evaluation is reviewing the purpose of, and circumstances that led to, the enactment of the PRA provisions and lessons learned from the banking and thrift crisis in the 1980s and early 1990s; evaluate to what extent PRA provisions were a factor in bank failures and problem institutions during the current crisis; and assess whether PRA provisions prompted federal regulators to act more quickly and more forcefully to limit losses to the DIF in the current crisis in light of lessons learned from the 1980s and early 1990s. We will also determine whether there are other non-capital measures that provide a leading indication of risks to the DIF that should be considered as part of PRA.

Office of Inspector General
Federal Housing Finance Agency

The Federal Housing Finance Agency Office of Inspector General (FHFA-OIG) began operations on October 12, 2010. Established by the Housing and Economic Recovery Act of 2008 (HERA), which amended the Inspector General Act, FHFA-OIG conducts, supervises, and coordinates audits, investigations, and other activities relating to the programs and operations of the Federal Housing Finance Agency (FHFA or the Agency), which regulates and supervises the housing-related Government-Sponsored Enterprises (GSEs): the Federal National Mortgage Association (Fannie Mae), the Federal Home Loan Mortgage Corporation (Freddie Mac) (collectively, the Enterprises), and the Federal Home Loan Banks (FHLBanks).

Although FHFA-OIG assumed its responsibilities only recently and has been primarily focused on building the organization, it has nonetheless recorded several significant accomplishments, including the release of three reports and significant participation in a major, ongoing mortgage fraud investigation. FHFA-OIG's *Inaugural Semiannual Report to the Congress*, published on May 26, 2011, and available at www.fhfaoig.gov, discusses FHFA's inception, initial accomplishments, and strategy in greater detail.

FHFA-OIG's Vision, Mission, and Core Values

FHFA-OIG's vision is to be an efficient and effective organization that promotes excellence and trust through its service to FHFA, Congress, the Administration, and the American public.

FHFA-OIG's mission is to:

- Promote the economy, efficiency, and effectiveness of FHFA's programs and operations;

- Prevent and detect fraud, waste, and abuse in the programs and operations of FHFA; and

- Seek administrative sanctions, civil recoveries, and/or criminal prosecutions of those responsible for fraud, waste, and abuse in connection with FHFA's programs and operations.

In carrying out its mission, FHFA-OIG:

- Keeps the Director of FHFA, Congress, and the American people fully and currently informed of problems and deficiencies relating to FHFA's programs and operations; and

- Works with FHFA staff and program participants to improve FHFA's programs and operations.

FHFA-OIG adheres to a defined set of core values:

Mission Driven. FHFA-OIG is committed to excellence with the aim of providing transparency and accountability in FHFA's programs and operations and improving its performance through measurable results;

Integrity. FHFA-OIG strives to maintain trust and integrity;

Professionalism. FHFA-OIG is committed to the highest standards of professional conduct;

Equal Employment Opportunity. FHFA-OIG promotes equal employment opportunity for all employees and job applicants; and

Confidentiality. FHFA-OIG is committed to maintaining the confidentiality of whistleblowers and others.

Leadership and Organizational Structure

The first FHFA Inspector General, Steve A. Linick, was nominated by President Barack Obama on April 12, 2010, confirmed by the United States Senate on September 29, 2010, and sworn into office on October 12, 2010. Prior to commencing service as the FHFA Inspector General, Mr. Linick served from 2006 to 2010 in several leadership positions at the U.S. Department of Justice. Previously, Mr. Linick was an Assistant United States Attorney, first in the Central District of California (1994-1999), and subsequently in the Eastern District of Virginia (1999-2006).

FHFA-OIG is comprised of the Inspector General, his Senior Staff, and the FHFA-OIG Offices. The Inspector General's Senior Staff includes the Chief of Staff, Chief Counsel, Director of External Affairs, and the Deputy Inspectors General for Audits, Evaluations, Investigations, and Administration. FHFA-OIG's principal operating Offices are the Office of Audits (OA), the Office of Evaluations (OE), and the Office of Investigations (OI). Offices with OIG-wide responsibilities are the Office of Counsel (OC), the Office of Policy, Oversight, and Review (OP), and the Office of Administration (OAd).

Office of Audits

OA provides audit and related services covering the programs and operations of FHFA. Through its financial and performance audits and attestation engagements, OA seeks to: (1) promote economy, efficiency, and effectiveness in the administration of FHFA's programs; (2) detect and deter fraud, waste, and abuse in FHFA's activities and operations; and (3) ensure compliance with applicable laws and regulations. Under the Inspector General Act, federal inspectors general are required to comply with standards established by the Comptroller General of the United States for audits of federal establishments, organizations, programs, activities, and functions. These standards, referred to as Generally Accepted Government Auditing Standards, are prescribed in the *Government Auditing Standards*, commonly referred to as the "Yellow Book." OA performs its audits and attestation engagements in accordance with applicable Generally Accepted Government Auditing Standards.

Office of Evaluations

OE reviews, studies, and analyzes FHFA's programmatic and operational activities and provides independent and objective analyses to FHFA. OE's evaluations are generally limited in scope and completed more quickly than traditional audits. When OE observes significant deficiencies in the effectiveness or efficiency of FHFA's programs and operations, it assists the Inspector General in developing recommendations to resolve them.

The Inspector General Reform Act of 2008 requires that federal inspectors general adhere to professional standards developed by the Council of the Inspectors General on Integrity and Efficiency (CIGIE). Evaluation standards are prescribed by CIGIE in its *Quality Standards for Inspection and Evaluation*, commonly referred to as the "Blue Book." OE performs its evaluations in accordance with these standards.

Office of Investigations

OI investigates allegations of misconduct or fraud involving the programs and operations of FHFA and the GSEs. OI Special Agents develop criminal and civil cases for referral to the U.S. Department of Justice and other law enforcement agencies.[21] OI adheres to CIGIE's *Quality Standards for Investigations* and fully complies with guidelines issued by the Attorney General. OI also generates administrative cases for presentation to FHFA and administers the FHFA-OIG Hotline, which can be reached at (800) 793-7724 or via email at OIGHOTLINE@FHFA.GOV. The Hotline provides concerned parties a way to report, directly and in confidence, information regarding possible fraud, waste, or abuse related to FHFA or the GSEs.

Office of Counsel

OC supports FHFA-OIG by providing independent legal advice, counseling, and opinions concerning FHFA-OIG's programs and operations. OC also reviews audit, investigation, and evaluation reports for legal sufficiency. It reviews drafts of FHFA regulations and policies and prepares comments as appropriate. OC also coordinates with the FHFA Office of General Counsel and manages FHFA-OIG's responses to requests and appeals made under the Freedom of Information Act and the Privacy Act.

Office of Policy, Oversight, and Review

OP provides advice, consultation, and assistance regarding FHFA-OIG's priorities, the scope of its evaluations and audits, and all reports published by FHFA-OIG. In addition, OP is responsible for conducting special studies and developing the Semiannual Report. Finally, OP plays an integral role in reviewing audits and evaluations and in identifying issues for review that are timely to FHFA, Congress, and the public.

Office of Administration

OAd is responsible for FHFA-OIG's human resources, budget development and execution, financial management, information technology, facilities and property management, safety, and continuity of operations.

Progress in Building FHFA-OIG Organization

Since beginning operations in October 2010 with no staff or infrastructure, FHFA-OIG has made significant progress in building its organization and capabilities, as detailed below.

Personnel

FHFA-OIG has over 70 full-time personnel, including seasoned investigators, evaluators, auditors, attorneys, subject matter experts, and administrative support staff.

---

21   On April 5, 2011, Attorney General Eric Holder authorized FHFA-OIG to exercise statutory law enforcement powers under the Inspector General Act.

Infrastructure

FHFA-OIG occupies the seventh floor of 1625 Eye Street, NW, Washington, DC. Many FHFA staff members occupy the third and fourth floors of the same building, and additional FHFA offices are nearby. FHFA (including FHFA-OIG) intends to consolidate in a new headquarters building in 2012.

FHFA-OIG's website (www.fhfaoig.gov) is now fully operational. FHFA-OIG posts all of its reports, testimony, and investigations (when permitted to be made available to the public) on the website as soon as possible.

Budget

Unlike most other federal agencies, FHFA and FHFA-OIG are not funded through Congressional appropriations. Rather, under HERA, FHFA and FHFA-OIG are funded through the collection of annual assessments levied on the GSEs. For fiscal year 2011, $29 million was assessed to fund the operations of FHFA-OIG.

FHFA-OIG Audits and Evaluations

Audit and Evaluation Activities to Date

To date, FHFA-OIG has released three public reports, which are briefly summarized below.

Federal Housing Finance Agency's Exit Strategy and Planning Process for the Enterprises' Structural Reform, EVL-2011-001, March 31, 2011

In an evaluation issued on March 31, 2011, FHFA-OIG found that FHFA would need to develop a careful planning strategy to implement the recommended actions in the Administration's February 11, 2011, housing finance system reform plan. The FHFA-OIG report identified the actions FHFA would be expected to take under the plan, such as requiring Fannie Mae and Freddie Mac to raise their guarantee fees or down-payment requirements for mortgages they purchase. The report noted that such steps involve potential risks to housing finance if not managed carefully. For example, raising the two GSEs' guarantee fees and underwriting standards too quickly could unnecessarily restrict the availability of mortgage credit. Careful planning by FHFA would require it to, among other things, establish planning timelines and external reporting strategies to keep mortgage market participants, Congress, and others apprised of its activities and progress. The FHFA-OIG evaluation report also noted that FHFA faces challenges in hiring staff necessary to manage its role as conservator and regulator as well as additional responsibilities under the Administration's proposal. FHFA concurred with the report's recommendations that it take specific steps to help ensure the effective implementation of FHFA's responsibilities, including: (1) establishing timeframes and milestones, descriptions of methodologies to be used, criteria for evaluating the implementation of the initiatives, and budget and financing information necessary to carry out its responsibilities; and (2) developing an external reporting strategy, which might include the augmentation of existing reports, to chronicle FHFA's progress, including the adequacy of its resources and capacity to meet multiple responsibilities and mitigate any shortfalls.

Evaluation of Federal Housing Finance Agency's Oversight of Fannie Mae's and Freddie Mac's Executive Compensation Programs, EVL-2011-002, March 31, 2011

In an evaluation report issued on March 31, 2011, FHFA-OIG found that FHFA did not have adequate processes in place to manage executive compensation programs for the senior officers at Fannie Mae and Freddie Mac. As conservator, FHFA can appoint senior officers and has the authority to review and approve their compensation packages. The top six senior officers at Fannie Mae and Freddie Mac received combined total compensation of $34.4 million in 2009 and 2010 under FHFA-approved compensation packages, and Agency officials believe such compensation is necessary to recruit and retain senior officers. However, FHFA-OIG found that FHFA had not considered factors that might have resulted in reduced executive compensation costs, such as the impact that federal financial support has on corporate executive performance and the compensation paid to senior officials at federal entities that also play a critical role in housing finance. Further, FHFA-OIG found that FHFA had neither developed written criteria to assess executive compensation levels at Fannie Mae and Freddie Mac, nor required Agency staff to verify and test the means by which the two GSEs calculated their recommended compensation levels.

FHFA-OIG made the following recommendations based on its findings: (1) FHFA should establish an ongoing review and analysis process to include issues such as the influence of federal support for Fannie Mae and Freddie Mac and the compensation levels for the heads of housing-related federal entities; (2) FHFA should establish written criteria and procedures for reviewing performance data and conduct independent verification and testing of the basis for executive compensation levels (these factors may warrant lower compensation); and (3) FHFA should improve transparency by posting information to its website about executive compensation and providing links to the securities filings. While FHFA agreed with most of these recommendations, it did not agree with FHFA-OIG's recommendations to: (1) assess disparities in compensation among senior officials at Fannie Mae and Freddie Mac, FHFA, the Federal Housing Administration, and the Government National Mortgage Association; and (2) test and verify independently Fannie Mae's and Freddie Mac's annual salary recommendations for their individual executives.

Audit of the Federal Housing Finance Agency's Consumer Complaints Process, AUD-2011-001, June 21, 2011

In an audit report issued on June 21, 2011, FHFA-OIG found that FHFA did not adequately process consumer complaints. The current national housing finance crisis has left millions of existing borrowers, communities, and investors struggling with delinquent and defaulted mortgages, loan modifications, and foreclosures. At the same time, consumers suffering from the effects of the crisis increasingly filed complaints with the Enterprises and FHFA, the conservator and regulator of the Enterprises. FHFA staff estimated that 70% - 75% of all complaints filed with the Agency pertained to the Enterprises. In light of these events, Congress and others expressed interest in whether FHFA adequately responded to consumer complaints including, but not limited to, complaints of fraud, waste, or abuse. These complaints run the gamut from difficulties obtaining information from the Enterprises to allegations of potential criminal activity. FHFA-OIG initiated an audit to assess how FHFA processed consumer complaints.

FHFA-OIG determined that FHFA did not: (1) sufficiently define its role in processing complaints; (2) develop and maintain a consolidated system for receiving and processing complaints; (3) establish effective procedures for evaluating and referring complaints alleging potential criminal conduct; (4) consistently follow up on complaints; (5) comply with its records management policy; (6) perform routine substantive analyses to identify overall trends; (7) implement necessary safeguards for personally identifiable information; or (8) prioritize complaints or assess the timeliness of responses to complainants. These deficiencies occurred because FHFA did not establish a sound internal control environment governing consumer complaints. Specifically, FHFA did not assign the complaint processing function sufficient priority, did not allocate adequate resources to the function, and did not provide effective oversight, including performance reporting on the resolution of complaints.

FHFA concurred with the report's recommendations that it: (1) design and implement written policies, procedures, and controls governing the receipt, processing, and disposition of consumer complaints and allegations of fraud, that among other things define the related roles and responsibilities for FHFA and the Enterprises, and provide for consultation with FHFA-OIG to process allegations of fraud; (2) assess the sufficiency of resources allocated to the complaints process; and (3) determine whether there are unresolved complaints alleging fraud or other potential criminal activity.

Audit and Evaluation Plan

FHFA-OIG has created a detailed audit and evaluation plan that focuses strategically on the areas of FHFA's operations that pose the greatest risks and provide the greatest potential benefits to FHFA, Congress, and the public. The current plan was developed based on an independent third-party risk assessment, reviews of relevant reports and documentation, and interviews with FHFA officials, Members of Congress, and others.[22]

Key aspects of the plan include reviews of FHFA's:

- Regulatory efforts and its management of the Fannie Mae and Freddie Mac conservatorships. Areas of focus include FHFA staff capacity, executive compensation, mortgage buyback settlements, foreclosure prevention and loss mitigation efforts, mortgage loan servicing controls, foreclosed property management and sales processes, model validation and risk-based guarantee pricing, and payment of legal fees. These are particularly high-risk areas because Treasury has invested over $162 billion of taxpayer funds (as of June 2011) in Fannie Mae and Freddie Mac. FHFA must regulate and supervise these organizations in an efficient, effective, and transparent manner so as to minimize taxpayer costs, conserve resources, and meet all statutory mandates;

- Oversight of the FHLBanks and their associated risks, including investment portfolio management, concentrations, and credit underwriting and administration;

- Oversight of the GSEs' housing missions, including affordable housing programs; and

- Internal operations, such as information security, privacy, and the handling of consumer complaints and allegations of fraud, waste, and abuse.

The Audit and Evaluation Plan identifies a number of other ongoing and planned reviews of specific FHFA programs and activities that fall into each of the risk areas. The following summarizes some of the projects that are currently in the plan.

FHFA's Oversight and Conservatorships of Fannie Mae and Freddie Mac
FHFA's Independence: This project will examine FHFA's independence and the processes it uses in exercising its decision-making authority, particularly in light of its multiple responsibilities. For example, FHFA has statutory obligations both to act as conservator for Fannie Mae and Freddie Mac and to support the housing finance system, which often includes Treasury's mortgage loan modification programs. FHFA-OIG

---

22 FHFA-OIG's plan is dynamic and will be revised as necessary.

will assess whether balancing potentially competing responsibilities may test FHFA's capacity going forward and its ultimate effectiveness.

FHFA's Oversight of Fannie Mae's Network of Foreclosure Processing Attorneys: Concerns have emerged that many foreclosures in recent years may not have been conducted according to state laws and regulations, which may have resulted in individuals and families losing their homes improperly. This project will assess FHFA's oversight of Fannie Mae's selection, management, and oversight of foreclosure attorney networks. Future work may also address FHFA's oversight of Freddie Mac's attorney networks.

FHFA's Review and Approval of Freddie Mac's Settlement with Bank of America Relating to Mortgage Buybacks: FHFA recently approved three settlements for approximately $3 billion between Fannie Mae and Freddie Mac, on the one hand, and Ally Financial (formerly GMAC) and Bank of America on the other, relating to Ally Financial's and Bank of America's buyback obligations. This project will assess FHFA's review and approval process for the settlement between Freddie Mac and Bank of America.

FHFA's Oversight of Fannie Mae's Loss Management Practices: As conservator, FHFA must preserve and conserve the assets of Fannie Mae and Freddie Mac, including minimizing losses. This project will assess FHFA's oversight of Fannie Mae's loan loss analyses used to determine the least costly approach to addressing seriously delinquent loans.

FHFA's Oversight of Enterprise Real Estate Owned Contractors: Fannie Mae and Freddie Mac engage contractors to handle the management and disposition of their portfolios of Real Estate Owned (REO). These activities can significantly impact the sales proceeds received. This project will assess FHFA's oversight of Fannie Mae's and Freddie Mac's controls over REO contractors engaged to manage and market single-family residential properties.

Federal Home Loan Banks

FHFA's Oversight of Troubled FHLBanks: Several FHLBanks face financial challenges due to their investments in private-label MBS, including those collateralized by subprime mortgages that have been impacted by the decline in housing values. This project will assess the steps that FHFA is taking to help ensure that these troubled FHLBanks return to financial soundness.

FHFA's Examinations of FHLBank Advance and Collateral Management Practices: FHLBank advances to their member financial institutions are secured by pledged collateral, such as single-family residential mortgages. Due to the dramatic decline in housing values in recent years, concerns have arisen about the value of collateral securing advances and the FHLBanks' collateral management practices. Further, as stated in an independent risk assessment commissioned by FHFA-OIG, some FHLBanks face substantial credit risks due to their relatively large advances to a small number of very large financial institutions. This project will assess FHFA's oversight of the FHLBanks' controls over underwriting standards and their compliance with such standards relative to credit decisions for advances and collateral verification.

FHFA Operations

FHFA's Implementation of Information Security Requirements: The Federal Information System Management Act of 2002 (FISMA) requires federal agencies, including FHFA, to have an annual independent evaluation of their information security program and practices and to report the results of the evaluation to the Office of Management and Budget. FISMA states that the independent evaluation is to be performed by the agency Inspector General or an independent external auditor, as determined by the Inspector General. This audit will assess FHFA's information security program and practices to determine whether they meet the security responsibilities outlined in FISMA.

FHFA-OIG Investigations

Investigations Activities to Date

FHFA-OIG has made a significant contribution to the investigation and prosecution of fraud involving Colonial Bank and Taylor, Bean & Whitaker Mortgage Corporation (TBW), which, to date, has resulted in the conviction of seven defendants. TBW was servicing $51 billion in Freddie Mac loans when it ceased operations in August 2009. Freddie Mac suffered significant economic losses as a result of this fraud.

TBW was one of the largest privately-held mortgage lending companies in the United States. TBW originated, purchased, sold, and serviced residential mortgage loans. TBW also pooled loans that it originated as collateral for mortgage-backed securities guaranteed by Freddie Mac and Ginnie Mae.

Beginning in early 2002, TBW began to experience significant cash flow problems. In an effort to cover these shortfalls, a group of conspirators devised various schemes that involved defrauding, among others, Colonial Bank (which provided short term funding to mortgage lending companies like TBW), Ocala Funding LLC (Ocala), a TBW special purpose entity, and U.S. taxpayers. By the middle of 2009, the conspirators had diverted nearly $3 billion from Colonial Bank and Ocala; attempted to misappropriate over $500 million from Treasury; and filed numerous false records with Freddie Mac, Ginnie Mae, and the Securities and Exchange Commission. Additionally, the conspirators allegedly covered up the diversions by selling loans owned by Colonial Bank to Freddie Mac without paying Colonial Bank for the loans. As a result, the conspirators caused Freddie Mac and Colonial Bank to believe that each had an undivided ownership interest in thousands of the same loans. TBW and Colonial Bank both failed in 2009. Freddie Mac reported substantial losses.

FHFA-OIG's investigation partners in this matter include the Office of the Special Inspector General for the Troubled Asset Relief Program, the Federal Bureau of Investigation, the Office of Inspector General for the Federal Deposit Insurance Corporation, the Office of Inspector General for the U.S. Department of Housing and Urban Development, and Internal Revenue Service – Criminal Investigation. The Financial Crimes Enforcement Network also provided investigative support. Additionally, the cases are being prosecuted by the Fraud Section of the Criminal Division at the U.S. Department of Justice and the United States Attorney for the Eastern District of Virginia.

In addition to the TBW matter, FHFA-OIG and its law enforcement partners are engaged in a number of non-public investigations. FHFA-OIG intends to develop further its close working relationships with other law enforcement agencies, including the U. S. Department of Justice, the United States Attorney's Offices, the Financial Crimes Enforcement Network, the Mortgage Fraud Working Group, the United States Secret Service, the Federal Bureau of Investigation, the Office of Inspector General for the U.S. Department of Housing and Urban Development, the Office of Inspector General for the Federal Deposit Insurance Corporation, Internal Revenue Service – Criminal Investigation, the Office of the Special Inspector General for the Troubled Asset Relief Program, and other federal, state, and local agencies. In addition, FHFA-OIG has undertaken law enforcement outreach efforts to United States Attorney's Offices across the nation, as well as a number of state Attorneys General.

FHFA-OIG Regulatory Review

Consistent with the Inspector General Act, FHFA-OIG considers whether proposed legislation and regulations related to FHFA are effective, efficient, economical, legal, and susceptible to fraud and abuse. Pursuant to its statutory authority, FHFA-OIG will continue to review all proposed FHFA rules to ensure their compliance with established requirements. FHFA-OIG will make recommendations to FHFA as deemed necessary and monitor its compliance with recommended courses of action.

To date, FHFA-OIG has reviewed 26 new or proposed FHFA policies and regulations and provided substantive comments on 10.

Office of Inspector General
National Credit Union Administration

Background

The National Credit Union Administration (NCUA) is responsible for chartering, insuring, and supervising Federal credit unions and administering the National Credit Union Share Insurance Fund (NCUSIF). The NCUA also administers the Community Development Revolving Loan Fund and manages the Central Liquidity Facility (CLF), a mixed-ownership government corporation the purpose of which is to supply emergency loans to member credit unions.

The 1988 amendments to the Inspector General Act of 1978 (IG Act), 5 U.S.C. App. 3, established IGs in 33 designated Federal entities (DFEs), including the NCUA.[23] The NCUA Office of Inspector General (OIG) was established in 1989. The NCUA IG is appointed by, reports to, and is under the general supervision of, a three-member presidentially-appointed Board. The OIG staff consists of nine FTEs: the IG, the Deputy IG, the Counsel to the IG; four senior auditors, one investigator, and an office manager. The OIG promotes the economy, efficiency, and effectiveness of NCUA programs and operations, and detects and deters fraud, waste and abuse, thereby supporting the NCUA's mission of facilitating the availability of credit union services to all eligible consumers through a regulatory environment that fosters a safe and sound credit union system. The OIG supports this mission by conducting independent audits, investigations, and other activities, and by keeping the NCUA Board and the Congress fully and currently informed of its work.

Role In Financial Oversight

With the ongoing challenges facing the entire financial services industry, the OIG's oversight of the NCUA has resulted in unprecedented levels of audit engagement and activity. In particular, the current economic environment has required the redirection of most of the OIG's audit resources to conducting material loss reviews (MLRs). The *Federal Credit Union Act* (FCUA), 12 U.S.C. 1790d(j), requires that the OIG conduct a MLR when the NCUSIF has incurred a material loss with respect to a credit union. A material loss is defined as (1) exceeding the sum of $25 million[24] and (2) an amount equal to 10% of the total assets of the credit union at the time at which the Board initiated assistance or was appointed liquidating agent. While the requirement for the NCUA IG to conduct MLRs was added to the FCUA with the passage of the *Credit Union Membership Access Act* in 1998, it was not until 2008—at the inception of the nation's financial downturn--that the OIG received its first MLR referrals. Since 2008, the NCUA OIG has completed 13 MLRs (10 natural person credit

---

23   5 U.S.C. App. 3, §8G.

24   Prior to the implementation of the "Dodd-Frank Wall Street Reform and Consumer Protection Act," ("Dodd-Frank") P.L. No. 111-203, 124 Stat. 1376 (2010), the monetary loss threshold was $10 million. As of July 2010, Section 988(a)(2)(A) of Dodd-Frank amended section 216(j) (12 U.S.C. 1790d(j)) of the FCUA to raise the threshold to $25 million.

unions and three corporate credit unions), is in the process of conducting four MLRs (two natural person credit unions and two corporate credit unions), and anticipates conducting five additional MLRs in 2011.

The NCUA OIG conducts MLRs to ascertain the reason for the loss to the NCUSIF; determine the reason for the credit union's failure, if there was a failure;[25] and assess NCUA's supervision of the credit union. Moreover, with the passage of Dodd-Frank, the NCUA OIG must determine--for losses that do not meet the statutory materiality threshold--whether any unusual circumstances exist that might warrant an in-depth OIG review regardless of the loss amount. In MLR reports, the OIG endeavors to provide constructive recommendations and/or exemplify lessons learned so that NCUA managers can provide better oversight and improve examiner supervision of credit unions. By offering these recommendations and lessons learned, the NCUA OIG assists the agency in its efforts to ensure that similar mistakes or shortcomings are not repeated in the future.

Material Loss Review Work

Corporate Credit Union MLRs

The FCUA authorizes natural person credit unions (NPCUs) to invest in shares or deposits of any central credit union (corporate credit union). 12 U.S.C. 1757(7)(G). A corporate credit union is an organization, chartered under the FCUA or under applicable state law as a credit union that receives shares from and provides loan and other services primarily to other credit unions. Historically, corporate credit unions have fulfilled an important role in the credit union industry and have provided credit unions with payment and clearing services, including access to wire transfer facilities and automated clearing house transactions. Corporate credit unions also provide investment services, enabling smaller credit unions to achieve economies of scale and access to greater market returns otherwise unavailable to them. Corporate credit unions likewise serve as an important source of liquidity for credit unions--through short and medium term credit facilities--and serve as agents on behalf of NCUA's CLF, in connection with loans funded by the CLF. Corporate credit unions also provide other operational services, such as coin and currency services and safekeeping of investments.

Because corporate credit unions provide vital investment, liquidity, and payment system services to NPCUs, they are integral to the overall stability of the credit union system. Many NPCUs, especially those of smaller asset size, would face significant challenges without the services and assistance provided by corporate credit unions. Beginning in mid-2007, corporate credit unions began to experience catastrophic reductions in the value of their investment portfolios. Those reductions, coupled with the virtual freeze-up of the market for trading in certain types of investment securities, dramatically undermined the stability of the corporate system overall.

In the aftermath of the NCUA's conservatorship of two major corporate credit unions-- -- U.S. Central Federal Credit Union (U.S. Central) and Western Corporate Federal Credit Union (WesCorp)—the OIG initiated MLRs to determine why both ultimately failed and to assess the agency's supervision of them.[26] As might be expected, due to their size and the massive losses both incurred, these two MLRs garnered significant public,

---

25 Unlike the material loss provision in section 38(k) of the "Federal Deposit Insurance Act," the requirement for the NCUA OIG to conduct a MLR is not contingent upon the financial institution's (here, credit union) failure. Rather, the triggering factor is the amount of the loss to the NCUSIF.

26 http://www.ncua.gov/Resources/OIG/Files/Reports/2010/OIG-10-17_MLR_USCentral_10.18.10.pdf http://www.ncua.gov/Resources/OIG/Files/Reports/2010/OIG-10-19MLRWesCorp_11.16.2010.pdf

Congressional, and industry-wide attention. The MLRs for U.S. Central and WesCorp, as well as the agency's response to the recommendations set forth in the MLRs, are discussed briefly below.

U.S. Central

The MLR found that U.S. Central's management and Board of Directors contributed directly to the corporate's failure and the resulting material losses--amounting to over $1.45 billion--to the NCUSIF and the Temporary Corporate Credit Union Stabilization Fund (TCCUSF). Specifically, the review found that U.S. Central failed due to losses associated with an excessive concentration of private label subprime and ALT-A mortgage-backed securities that deteriorated in value following the mortgage-backed securities market dislocation in mid-2007. The MLR also documented U.S. Central's aggressive growth strategy that led to the purchase of excessive concentrations of high risk, higher yielding mortgage-backed securities with inadequate governance over these investment activities.

With regard to NCUA's supervisory actions, the MLR determined that the agency failed to adequately identify and timely focus on U.S. Central's investment portfolio until it was much too late. The review partially attributed NCUA's lack of adequate and timely oversight of U.S. Central to NCUA examiners not having the appropriate regulatory support, such as more specific investment concentration limits, to adequately address U.S. Central's increasing concentration risk and the increasing exposure to credit, market, and liquidity risks.

WesCorp

The OIG's MLR determined that WesCorp's management and Board of Directors did not implement appropriate risk management practices to adequately limit or control significant risks in its investment strategy. The review revealed that although WesCorp invested in high investment grade securities (AAA and AA), the Board and management implemented an aggressive investment strategy with unreasonable limits in place that allowed for excessive investments in privately-issued residential mortgage backed securities (RMBS). The substantial investment portfolio of privately-issued RMBS, resulting in a significant concentration risk, left WesCorp increasingly vulnerable to significant credit risk, market risk, and liquidity risk through the portfolio's exposure to worsening economic conditions in the residential real estate sector. The MLR report concluded that WesCorp management's actions contributed directly to conditions that resulted in WesCorp's liquidation in October 2010 and a loss of over $5 billion.

The MLR also determined that NCUA did not adequately and aggressively address WesCorp's increasing concentration of privately-issued RMBS and the increasing exposure of WesCorp's balance sheet to credit, market, and liquidity risks. Specifically, the review found that examiners did not question or respond in a timely manner to WesCorp's growing concentrations of privately-issued RMBS. As with U.S. Central, the MLR noted that NCUA did not have appropriate regulatory support available, in the form of more specific investment concentration limits, to address the growing and risky investment concentration. Consequently, the review concluded, agency examiners did not have the regulatory leverage to limit or stop the growth of WesCorp's purchase of privately-issued RMBS. The OIG opined in the MLR that such regulatory leverage would have likely mitigated WesCorp's severely distressed financial condition and expected loss and, consequently, averted NCUA's conservatorship of WesCorp.

NCUA Response to Corporate Credit Union MLRs

To respond to the overall crisis in the corporate credit union system, as well as to address the specific recommendations the OIG set forth in the U.S. Central and WesCorp MLRs, the NCUA developed a Corporate

System Resolution (CSR) plan. The CSR plan consists of a comprehensive 3-Phase Stabilize, Resolve, and Reform Strategy that has four guiding principles: (1) prevent interruption of payment services to credit unions and the ninety million credit union consumers; (2) preserve confidence in the credit union system; (3) manage to the least long-term cost consistent with sound public policy; and (4) facilitate an orderly transition to a new regulatory regime and future state for the corporate credit union system.

As part of the Reform phase of the CSR plan, the NCUA revised extensively its rule governing corporates and related rule provisions.[27] NCUA stated that its intent in establishing the new rule was twofold: to design a corporate rule that would prevent the catastrophic losses that occurred in the corporate system beginning in 2007 from ever recurring, and to allow for the survival of some form of a well-run corporate system that could provide necessary services, including payments systems services to its members and build and attract sufficient capital. The rule amendments established a new capital scheme for corporates, including risk-based capital requirements; imposed new prompt corrective actions; placed various new limits on corporate investments (including prohibiting corporates from purchasing either private label RMBS, or subordinated-type securities, going forward); imposed new asset-liability management controls; amended some corporate governance provisions; and limited a corporate CUSO to categories of services pre-approved by NCUA.

Concurrently, as part of its resolution plan, NCUA created two bridge corporate credit unions to assume operations of U.S. Central and WesCorp. The focus of the bridge corporates is to facilitate payments and settlement activities to ensure uninterrupted member services. The bridge corporates will operate for a targeted 24 months to allow member credit unions to orderly transition to alternative service providers.

Finally, NCUA recently issued additional final amendments to its rule governing corporate credit unions.[28] These amendments include internal control and reporting requirements for corporates similar to those required for banks under the *Federal Deposit Insurance Act* and the *Sarbanes-Oxley Act*. The amendments also require corporate credit unions to establish an enterprise-wide risk management committee staffed with a risk management expert, conduct all board of director votes as recorded votes, and disclose certain credit union service organization (CUSO) compensation received by employees who are dual employees of corporates and corporate CUSOs. It also permits corporates to charge reasonable one-time or periodic membership fees as necessary to facilitate retained earnings growth.

Other MLR Work

In addition to the MLRs it conducted on corporate credit unions, the OIG has also, since 2008, dedicated significant time and resources to conducting MLRs on NPCUs. In November 2010, the OIG issued a capping report that summarized significant findings from the first ten MLR reports issued, as well recommendations for avoiding similar mistakes and shortcomings in the future.[29]

The capping report found that, overwhelmingly, the actions of credit union management contributed significantly to the failures and ensuing losses to the NCUSIF. In particular, the OIG found the following

---

27   http://www.ncua.gov/Resources/RegulationsOpinionsLaws/final/FederalRegisterCorpCUFinalRule.pdf

28   http://www.ncua.gov/Resources/RegulationsOpinionsLaws/final/76FR23861[2011-10108]_CorpCUs.pdf

29   http://www.ncua.gov/Resources/OIG/Files/Reports/2010/OIG-10-20OIGCappingReportMLRs_11.23.10.pdf

recurring problems that credit union management was either unwilling or unable to effectively manage or mitigate:

- Poor strategic planning and decision making

- Inadequate oversight (policies and internal controls)

- Fraud

These shortcomings and failures on credit union management's part, the OIG concluded, exposed the credit unions to significant amounts of risk.

With regard to NCUA's actions, the OIG made 12 specific recommendations to the agency to address these problem areas. Since the capping report was issued, the NCUA has provided the OIG with a detailed chronology of corrective actions it has already taken to address each of the recommendations, as well as corrective actions in progress and anticipated, along with targeted completion dates.

Overall Recommendations

The overarching purpose of the OIG's audit and MLR work is to translate its findings into recommendations to improve NCUA's examination process and supervision efforts. With such improvements, the NCUA can then better identify and address problems before they result in either a loss to the NCUSIF or the failure of a credit union. In this regard, the OIG intends to continue its oversight work to assist the NCUA in proactively identifying areas of concern and implementing corrective actions in a timely manner. In general, the OIG recommends that the NCUA continue to pursue the following actions that it is already in the process of implementing or plans to take in the near future:

- Strengthening the NCUA risk-based examination program to require annual examinations of every federal credit union and increased on-site reviews of state-chartered credit unions.

- Taking stronger resolution action earlier in the process when problems are identified.

- Providing stronger regulation and supervision relative to interest rate risk management.

- Acquiring additional specialized expertise and incorporating enhanced training programs for examination staff.

- Implementing additional proactive risk management programs.

- Pursuing statutory changes to its enabling statute, the FCUA, as necessary, to enhance its ability to serve as an effective safety and soundness regulator of over 7,400 credit unions and deposit insurer for 90 million members.

Office of Inspector General
Securities and Exchange Commission

Agency Overview

The mission of the United States Securities and Exchange Commission (SEC or Commission) is to protect investors; maintain fair, orderly, and efficient markets; and facilitate capital formation. The SEC strives to promote a market environment that is worthy of the public's trust and characterized by transparency and integrity. The SEC's core values consist of integrity, accountability, effectiveness, teamwork, fairness, and commitment to excellence. The SEC's goals are to foster and enforce compliance with the federal securities laws; establish an effective regulatory environment; facilitate access to the information investors need to make informed investment decisions; and enhance the Commission's performance through effective alignment and management of human resources, information, and financial capital.

SEC staff monitor and regulate a securities industry that includes more than 35,000 registrants, including over 10,000 public companies, about 11,500 investment advisers, about 7,800 mutual funds, and about 5,400 broker-dealers, as well as national securities exchanges and self-regulatory organizations, 600 transfer agents, the Municipal Securities Rulemaking Board, the Public Company Accounting Oversight Board, alternate trading systems, and credit rating agencies.

The SEC is organized into five main divisions—Corporation Finance (CF); Enforcement; Investment Management (IM); Trading and Markets (TM); and Risk, Strategy, and Financial Innovation—and 16 functional offices. The Commission has its headquarters in Washington, D.C., and 11 regional offices located throughout the country. As of September 30, 2010, the SEC employed 3,748 full-time equivalents, consisting of 3,664 permanent and 84 temporary full-time equivalents.

Mission of the SEC OIG

The role of the SEC Office of Inspector General (OIG) is to promote the integrity, efficiency, and effectiveness of the critical programs and operations of the SEC, as described above. This mission is best achieved by having an effective, vigorous, and independent office of seasoned and talented professionals who perform the following functions:

- conducting independent and objective audits, evaluations, investigations, and other reviews of SEC programs and operations;

- preventing and detecting fraud, waste, abuse, and mismanagement in SEC programs and operations;

- identifying vulnerabilities in SEC systems and operations and recommending constructive solutions;

- offering expert assistance to improve SEC programs and operations;

- communicating timely and useful information that facilitates management decision making and the achievement of measurable gains; and

- keeping the Commission and the Congress fully and currently informed of significant issues and developments.

Inspector General H. David Kotz was appointed in December 2007, and since that time the office has issued numerous detailed audit and investigative reports discussing issues critical to SEC operations and the investing public and making significant recommendations for improvement. Some examples of the work performed by the SEC OIG concerning financial oversight activities are described in detail below.

Recent Examples of Oversight Work Performed by SEC OIG

Audits and Investigations Related to the Failure of the SEC to Uncover Bernard Madoff's Ponzi Scheme

On December 11, 2008, the SEC charged Bernard Madoff with securities fraud for a multi-billion dollar Ponzi scheme that he perpetrated on advisory clients of his firm. The complaint charged Madoff with violations of the anti-fraud provisions of the Securities Act of 1933, the Securities Exchange Act of 1934 (Exchange Act), and the Investment Advisers Act of 1940. In addition, the U.S. Attorney's Office in the Southern District of New York indicted Madoff for criminal offenses on the same date. On March 12, 2009, Madoff pled guilty to all charges and on June 29, 2009, U.S. District Judge Denny Chin sentenced Madoff to serve 150 years in prison, which was the maximum sentence allowed.

By mid-December 2008, the SEC learned that credible and specific allegations regarding Madoff's financial wrongdoing had been repeatedly brought to the attention of SEC staff but were never recommended to the Commission for action. As a result, on the late evening of December 16, 2008, former SEC Chairman Christopher Cox[30] contacted the SEC OIG asking us to undertake an investigation into allegations made to the SEC regarding Madoff, going back to at least 1999, and the reasons that these allegations were found to be not credible. Former Chairman Cox also asked that the OIG investigate the SEC's internal policies that govern when allegations of fraudulent activity should be brought to the Commission. In addition, he requested that the OIG investigation include all staff contact and relationships with the Madoff family and firm, and any impact such relationships had on staff decisions regarding the firm.

The SEC OIG thus conducted a large-scale investigation concentrating on the issues set forth in former Chairman Cox's request for an investigation, as well as two targeted audits. These audits were designed to assess the adequacy of examinations conducted by the SEC's Office of Compliance Inspections and Examinations (OCIE) in response to complaints regarding the activities of Madoff and his investment firm, and to identify systemic issues that would prevent the SEC's Division of Enforcement (Enforcement) from accomplishing its mission to enforce the securities laws and protect investors and determine from discussions with staff and supervisors which programmatic improvements are needed. A detailed description of the investigative and audit review work conducted by the SEC OIG follows.

---

30 Chairman Cox resigned on January 20, 2009. Current SEC Chairman Mary Schapiro was appointed by President Barack Obama on January 20, 2009, and was sworn in on January 27, 2009.

SEC OIG Office of Investigations, Case No. OIG-509: Investigation of Failure of the SEC to Uncover Bernard Madoff's Ponzi Scheme

Initiated at the request of former SEC Chairman Christopher Cox as described above, the OIG's investigation of the SEC's failure to uncover Madoff's Ponzi scheme analyzed the SEC's response to all complaints it received regarding the activities of Madoff, and traced the path of these complaints through the Commission from inception, reviewing what investigative or examination work was conducted with respect to these allegations. Further, we assessed the conduct of examinations and/or investigations of Madoff and/or Bernard Madoff Investment Securities, LLC (BMIS), by the SEC and conducted an analysis of whether there were "red flags" that were overlooked by SEC examiners or investigators (which may have been identified by other entities conducting due diligence) that could have led to a more comprehensive examination or investigation. We also considered the extent to which the reputation and status of Madoff and the fact that he served on SEC advisory committees, participated on securities industry boards and panels, and had social and professional relationships with SEC officials may have affected Commission decisions regarding investigations, examinations, and inspections of his firm.

The OIG's investigation was conducted over the course of nine months, with a 457-page report of investigation being issued on August 31, 2009. During the course of the investigation, the OIG estimates that it obtained and searched approximately 3.7 million e-mails and conducted 140 testimonies and interviews of 122 individuals with knowledge relevant to the investigation. The OIG investigation found that the SEC received more than ample information in the form of detailed and substantive complaints over the years to warrant a thorough and comprehensive examination and/or investigation of Madoff and BMIS for operating a Ponzi scheme, and that despite three examinations and two investigations being conducted, a thorough and competent investigation or examination was never performed. The OIG found that between June 1992 and December 2008, when Madoff confessed, the SEC received six substantive complaints that raised significant red flags concerning Madoff's hedge fund operations and should have led to questions about whether Madoff was actually engaged in trading. Finally, the SEC was also aware of two articles regarding Madoff's investment operations that appeared in reputable publications in 2001 and questioned Madoff's unusually consistent returns.

The complaints all contained specific information and could not have been fully and adequately resolved without thoroughly examining and investigating Madoff for operating a Ponzi scheme. The journal articles should have reinforced the concerns about how Madoff could have been achieving his returns.

The OIG investigation further found that the SEC conducted two investigations and three examinations related to Madoff's investment advisory business based upon the detailed and credible complaints that raised the possibility that Madoff was misrepresenting his trading and could have been operating a Ponzi scheme. Yet at no time did the SEC ever verify Madoff's trading through an independent third party or actually conduct a Ponzi scheme examination or investigation of Madoff.

We also found that investors who may have been uncertain about whether to invest with Madoff were reassured by the fact that the SEC had investigated and/or examined Madoff, or entities that did business with Madoff, and had found no evidence of fraud. Moreover, we found that Madoff proactively informed potential investors that the SEC had examined his operations. When potential investors expressed hesitation about investing with Madoff, he cited the prior SEC examinations to establish credibility and allay suspicions or investor doubts that may have arisen while due diligence was being conducted. Thus, the fact that the

SEC had conducted examinations and investigations and did not detect the fraud lent credibility to Madoff's operations and had the effect of encouraging additional individuals and entities to invest with him.

The OIG investigation determined that despite numerous credible and detailed complaints, the SEC never properly examined or investigated Madoff's trading and never took the necessary, but basic, steps to determine if Madoff was operating a Ponzi scheme. Had these efforts been made with appropriate follow-up at any time beginning in June of 1992 until December 2008, the SEC could have uncovered the Ponzi scheme before Madoff confessed.

The OIG's full report can be found on the SEC's website at http://www.sec.gov/news/studies/2009/oig-509.pdf

SEC OIG Office of Audits, Report No. 468: Review and Analysis of OCIE Examinations of Bernard L. Madoff Investment Securities, LLC

On June 25, 2009, the SEC OIG retained the services of a team of experts at FTI Consulting, Inc. (FTI Engagement Team) to assess the adequacy of examinations conducted by OCIE in response to complaints regarding the activities of Madoff and his investment firm. The FTI Engagement Team found that OCIE examiners made critical mistakes in nearly every aspect of their examinations of Madoff and BMIS and missed significant opportunities to uncover Madoff's Ponzi scheme. The FTI Engagement Team concluded that OCIE examiners did not properly plan or conduct their examinations of Madoff and, because of these failures, were unable to discover Madoff's fraud.

The resulting report presented 37 specific and concrete recommendations designed to improve nearly every aspect of OCIE's operations. The following are summaries of many of our key recommendations:

We recommended that examiners be provided access to industry publications and databases and that protocols be established for analyzing information from these outside sources. The report recommended that OCIE establish a specific protocol that explains how to identify red flags and potential violations of securities laws based on the information gleaned from these sources.

We recommended that a collection system for capturing information in tips and complaints be implemented, institution of a requirement that OCIE annually review and test the effectiveness of the new system, and implementation of procedures to ensure that all OCIE-related tips and complaints are vetted within 30 days of receipt and that examinations commence within 60 days of receipt.

The report prescribed specific procedures regarding scope and planning memoranda for cause examinations, including a requirement of concurring review by an unaffiliated senior-level official. We also recommended that OCIE examiners be required to document all substantive interviews, prepare detailed workpapers, and log all examinations into a tracking system. We also made a number of concrete recommendations regarding the selection of the examination team.

We recommended that a formal plan be developed to ensure that within a three-year period, 50 percent of OCIE staff become qualified by means of an industry certification to conduct thorough and comprehensive examinations. The report also recommended the development of interactive exercises prior to hiring new OCIE examiners to evaluate the relevant skills necessary to perform examinations. Moreover, the report makes recommendations for training OCIE examiners in the mechanics of securities settlements and in regulations of foreign and domestic exchanges.

The report recommended that it be mandatory for OCIE staff to verify a sample of transactions with an independent third party and that the staff be given direct access to databases maintained by self-regulatory organizations to allow them to perform verifications of registrant information.

The report recommended requirements for all cause examinations to be tracked consistently and appropriately and for examinations to be concluded with a closing report.

The report recommended that OCIE management make clear that it will support OCIE examiners in their pursuit of evidence in the course of an examination.

OCIE concurred with all 37 of the OIG's recommendations. The OIG's full report can be found on the SEC's website at http://www.sec-oig.gov/Reports/AuditsInspections/2009/468.pdf

SEC OIG Office of Audits, Report No. 467: Program Improvements Needed Within the SEC's Division of Enforcement

In June 2009, as a result of issues identified during the OIG's investigation into the SEC's failure to uncover the Madoff Ponzi scheme, the OIG Office of Audits launched a survey questionnaire to Enforcement staff designed to identify systemic issues that would prevent Enforcement from accomplishing its mission to enforce the securities laws and protect investors. The survey was intended to obtain feedback on topics such as allocation of resources, performance measurement, case management procedures, communication, adequacy of policies and procedures, employee morale, and management efficiency and effectiveness.

The review found that several program improvements were needed within Enforcement with regard to complaint handling processes, fostering of relationships inside and outside the Division, verification of information with industry experts outside the Commission, timely handling of administrative matters related to opening and closing investigations, effective supervision over investigations, communication of program priorities, and case handling processes.

Specifically, we found that Enforcement staff lacked adequate guidance on how to appropriately analyze complaints. In addition, we found that Enforcement staff assigned to investigate Madoff were inexperienced and that the investigation suffered as a result of a lack of supervision. We also found that Enforcement staff did not always exercise due diligence in their handling of critical information regarding Madoff. Further, Enforcement staff investigating Madoff did not always seek assistance from other offices and divisions as needed during the investigation. Additionally, Enforcement staff working on the Madoff investigation failed to verify information provided by Madoff with independent third-party sources, a critical step in order to determine whether Madoff was actually engaged in trading. Furthermore, Enforcement staff did not adequately evaluate information received by the SEC while the Madoff investigation was inactive pending closure. Additionally, we found there were delays in completing administrative tasks related to opening a matter under inquiry on Madoff, as well as in closing the investigation.

In addition, based on our survey of management effectiveness in Enforcement, we found that a large number of Enforcement staff had concerns regarding working relationships within Enforcement, communication of program priorities, and case handling processes. Staff also expressed that they did not always know where to find information regarding impartiality in the performance of their duties.

To strengthen management controls in the Division, the OIG made 21 concrete recommendations to Enforcement, including the following:

- Establish formal guidance for evaluating various types of complaints (e.g , Ponzi schemes) and train appropriate staff on the use of the guidance.

- Ensure that the SEC's tip and complaint handling system provides for data capture of relevant information relating to the vetting process to document why a complaint was or was not acted upon and who made that determination.

- Require tips and complaints to be reviewed by at least two individuals experienced in the subject matter prior to deciding not to take further action.

- Establish guidance to require that all complaints that appear on the surface to be credible and compelling be probed further by in-depth interviews with the sources to assess the complaints' validity and to determine what issues need to be investigated.

Other recommendations concerned Enforcement's training of staff; annual review and testing of the effectiveness of Enforcement's new tip and complaint handling system; putting in place procedures to ensure that investigations are assigned to teams where at least one individual has specific and sufficient knowledge of the subject matter (e.g., Ponzi schemes) and the team has access to at least one additional individual who also has such expertise or knowledge; making it mandatory that planning memoranda be prepared during an investigation and that plans include specific information pertaining to scope, methodology, and expertise; and establishing procedures to enable junior-level Enforcement attorneys to escalate their concerns to senior-level management within Enforcement.

Enforcement concurred with all of the 21 recommendations included in the report. The OIG's full report can be found on the SEC's website at http://www.sec-oig.gov/Reports/AuditsInspections/2009/467.pdf

SEC OIG Office of Audits, Report No. 458: The SEC's Role Regarding and Oversight of Nationally Recognized Statistical Rating Organizations (NRSROs)

The Financial Crisis Inquiry Commission reported the following in January 2011:

> The three credit rating agencies were key enablers of the financial meltdown. The mortgage-related securities at the heart of the crisis could not have been marketed and sold without their seal of approval. Investors relied on them, often blindly. In some cases, they were obligated to use them, or regulatory capital standards were hinged on them. This crisis could not have happened without the rating agencies. Their ratings helped the market soar and their downgrades through 2007 and 2008 wreaked havoc across markets and firms.

The Dodd-Frank Wall Street Reform and Consumer Protection Act, enacted on July 21, 2010 (Dodd-Frank) significantly enhanced the SEC's enforcement mechanisms with regard to credit rating agencies and imposed a number of requirements on NRSROs that were immediately effective (i.e., did not depend on SEC rulemaking). Dodd-Frank also required the Commission to adopt a number of new rules concerning NRSROs.

A credit rating is an opinion issued by a credit rating agency (CRA), as of a specific date, of the creditworthiness (i.e., the ability to repay timely loan principal and interest) of an issuer or with respect to particular securities or money market instruments. The Commission specified in 1975 that a broker-dealer, in computing its net capital, could take a lesser deduction from its net worth as to securities rated as having a comparatively low chance of default according to a credit rating of national repute, or a "nationally recognized statistical rating organization" (NRSRO). Thereafter, the Commission incorporated the NRSRO concept into many rules and regulations issued under the federal securities laws, and the term was also used in a number of federal, state, and foreign laws and regulations.

The SEC OIG review focused on the SEC's implementation of and compliance with the Rating Agency Act and Commission rules. We also reviewed the Commission's history with NRSROs to assess the Commission's efforts to oversee the NRSROs and to implement the Rating Agency Act's accountability, competition, and transparency objectives. Our review determined that several improvements are needed to ensure compliance with the Rating Agency Act and the Commission's implementing regulations and to enhance NRSRO oversight.

In the report, we made several recommendations to TM designed to ensure compliance with the NRSRO application approval process established by the Rating Agency Act, including the following:

- Ensure that all significant issues identified in the application review process are resolved prior to TM recommending approval of the application by the Commission.

- In consultation with the appropriate offices, evaluate whether action should be taken regarding the CRA that was granted NRSRO designation despite the numerous significant problems identified with the application.

- Ensure that all pending issues previously identified during the NRSRO application process be resolved within six months of the date of the issuance of the report.

- In consultation with other appropriate offices, request that the Office of the General Counsel (OGC) develop guidance to assist TM in deciding under what circumstances it should seek consent from an applicant to waive the 90-day statutory time period for Commission action on an NRSRO application or recommend that the Commission institute proceedings to demine whether registration should be denied.

We also recommended, in order to ensure compliance with statutory and regulatory requirements pertaining to NRSROs, that TM do the following:

- Ensure in the future that it seeks Commission orders regarding NRSRO requests for extension of time when required by statute or the Commission's rules.

- Ensure that CRAs applying for NRSRO registration and firms that are registered as NRSROs comply with the Commission's rules and requirements regarding the filing and certification of financial information.

In addition, our review made several recommendations designed to improve the effectiveness of OCIE's NRSRO examination program, including the seeking of legislative authority to conduct examinations of CRAs as part of the NRSRO application process, the inclusion of NRSROs in OCIE's pilot monitoring program, and obtaining an additional review of OCIE's NRSRO examination module by someone with industry expertise.

With regard to the numerous NRSRO policy issues which our review found that the Commission should address to enhance its oversight of NRSROs, we made recommendations pertaining to

- seeking legislative authority to require that NRSRO auditors be subject to oversight by the Public Company Accounting Oversight Board (PCAOB);

- performing examination work regarding and assessing the adverse effect of the provision of consulting and advisory service on the quality of credit ratings;

- implementing a comprehensive credit rating monitoring requirement for NRSROs;

- performing examination work regarding and assessing undue influence on credit rating analysts and the benefits of an analyst rotation requirement;

- recommending additional disclosures about the credit ratings process;

- examining and assessing whether the revolving door problem is negatively impacting the quality of credit ratings;

- assessing the potential effects on competition in the credit rating industry of proposed amendments regarding the disclosure of material nonpublic information to other NRSROs, but not to CRAs that do not have NRSRO designation;

- recommending rules to reduce the potential harmful effects of forum shopping on the quality of credit ratings; and

- incorporating the seeking and consideration of public comments into the NRSRO oversight process.

Finally, we made several suggestions for including additional concepts identified by our review in the Commission's annual report to Congress regarding NRSROs.

The SEC Divisions and Offices concurred or partially concurred with 23 of the 24 recommendations in this report. The OIG's full report can be found on the SEC's website at http://www.sec-oig.gov/Reports/AuditsInspections/2009/Report458.pdf

SEC OIG Office of Audits, Report No. 474: Assessment of the SEC's Bounty Program

Dodd-Frank established a whistleblower program that requires the Commission to pay an award, under regulations prescribed by the Commission and subject to certain limitations, to eligible whistleblowers who voluntarily provide the Commission with original information about a violation of the federal securities laws that leads to the successful enforcement of a covered judicial or administrative action, or a related action. Dodd-Frank also prohibits retaliation by employers against individuals who provide the Commission with information about possible securities violations.

There is evidence that these types of bounty programs are an effective tool to encourage whistleblowers to come forward and provide necessary incentives for outside entities to bring complaints about possible illegal activity. Section 21A(e) of the Exchange Act, 18 U.S.C. § 78u-1(e), authorized the SEC to award a bounty to a person who provides information leading to the recovery of a civil penalty from an insider trader, from a person who tipped information to an insider trader, or from a person who directly or indirectly controlled an insider trader. All bounty determinations, including whether, to whom, or in what amount to make payments, are within the sole discretion of the SEC.

The SEC OIG conducted a review of the SEC bounty program to assess whether necessary management controls have been established and operate effectively to ensure that bounty applications are routed to appropriate personnel and are properly processed and tracked and to determine whether other government agencies with similar programs have best practices that could be incorporated into the SEC bounty program.

The SEC OIG found in its review that although the SEC had had a bounty program in-place for more than 20 years for rewarding whistleblowers for insider trading tips and complaints, very few payments had been made under this program. The OIG also found that the Commission had not received a large number of applications from individuals seeking a bounty over this 20-year period and that the program was not widely recognized inside or outside the Commission. Additionally, while the Commission recently asked for expanded authority from Congress to reward whistleblowers who bring forward substantial evidence about other significant federal securities law violations, we found that the SEC bounty program was not fundamentally well-designed to be successful.

More specifically, we found that improvements were needed to the bounty application process to make it more user-friendly and help ensure that bounty applications provide detailed information regarding the alleged securities law violations. We also found that the criteria for judging bounty applications were broad and the SEC had not put in place internal policies and procedures to assist staff in assessing contributions made by whistleblowers and making bounty award determinations. Additionally, we found that the Commission did not routinely provide status reports to whistleblowers regarding their bounty applications, even if a whistleblower's information led to an investigation. Moreover, we found that once bounty applications were received by the SEC and forwarded to appropriate staff for review and further consideration, they were not tracked to ensure that they were timely and adequately reviewed. Lastly, we found that files regarding bounty referrals did not always contain complete documentation, such as a copy of the bounty application, a memorandum sent to the whistleblower to acknowledge receipt of the application, and a referral memorandum showing the office or division and official to whom the bounty application was referred for further consideration.

As a result of this review, the OIG made 7 specific recommendations to Enforcement, including the following:

- Develop a communication plan to address outreach to both the public and SEC personnel regarding the SEC bounty program.

- Develop and post to Enforcement's public website an application form that asks the whistleblower to provide information.

- Establish policies on when to follow up with whistleblowers who submit applications to clarify information in the bounty applications and obtain readily available supporting documentation prior to making a decision as to whether a whistleblower's complaint should be further investigated.

- Develop specific criteria for recommending the award of bounties, including a provision that where a whistleblower relies partially upon public information, such reliance will not preclude the individual from receiving a bounty.

- Examine ways in which the Commission can increase communications with whistleblowers by notifying them of the status of their bounty requests without releasing nonpublic or confidential information during the course of an investigation or examination.

- Develop a plan to incorporate controls for tracking tips and complaints from whistleblowers seeking bounties into the development of Enforcement's tips, complaints, and referrals processes and systems for other tips and complaints.

Enforcement concurred with all of the 9 recommendations included in the report. The OIG's full report can be found on the SEC's website http://www.sec-oig.gov/Reports/AuditsInspections/2010/474.pdf

SEC OIG Office of Audits, Report No. 480: Review of the SEC's Section 13(f) Reporting Requirements

In 1975, Congress enacted Section 13(f) of the Exchange Act, 15 U.S.C. § 78m(f), to increase the public availability of information regarding the securities holdings of institutional investors. Section 13(f) and the Commission's implementing regulation require institutional investment managers that exercise investment discretion with respect to accounts holding certain equity securities having an aggregate fair market value of $100 million or more on the last trading day in a calendar year to file quarterly reports of their holdings with the SEC on Form 13F electronically through the Commission's Electronic Database Gathering and Retrieval (EDGAR) system. Under Commission Rule 13f-1, 17 C.F.R. § 240.13f-1, the Form 13F reports must be filed within 45 days after the last day of such calendar year and within 45 days after the last day of each of the first three calendar quarters of the subsequent calendar year. Section 13(f)(3) mandates that the Commission tabulate the information contained in the quarterly reports and disseminate that information to the public.

Lauding the beneficial disclosure provisions of the Dodd-Frank Act, SEC Chairman Mary Schapiro has stated, "This law creates a new, more effective regulatory structure, fills a host of regulatory gaps, brings greater public transparency and market accountability to the financial system and gives investors important protections and greater input into corporate governance." To that end, Section 766 of Dodd-Frank amended Section 13(f)(1)— which requires the filing of 13F reports— adding the following language with respect to who must file the reports: "or otherwise becomes or is deemed to become a beneficial owner of any security of a class described in subsection (d)(1) upon the purchase or sale of a security-based swap that the Commission may define by rule." On March 17, 2011, the SEC proposed to readopt portions of Rules 13d-3 and 16a-1 under the Exchange Act solely for the purpose of preserving the current treatment of security-based swap agreements under Sections 13(d), 13(g) and 16 of the Act.

Section 929X(a) of Dodd-Frank amended Section 13(f) to require the Commission to adopt rules requiring monthly (or potentially more frequent) public short sale disclosures by security, including the "aggregate amount of the number of short sales of each security, and any additional information determined by the Commission." The securities that must be reported under Section 13(f) generally include equity securities that are traded on an exchange or quoted on National Association of Securities Dealers Automated Quotations (NASDAQ), equity options and warrants, shares of closed-end investment companies, and some convertible debt securities. Under Section 13 (f)(3) of the Exchange Act, the Commission is responsible for publishing an official list of the securities that must be reported pursuant to Section 13(f)(1). Form 13F requires disclosure of the name and address of the institutional investment manager filing the report and, for each security being reported, specific information, including the name of the issuer, the class, the CUSIP number, the number of shares or principal amount, and the aggregate fair market value.

The OIG conducted a review to examine whether the Commission's implementation of and practices under Section 13(f) met Congress's intent in establishing Section 13(f), to examine the sufficiency of the Commission's existing policies and procedures that implement Section 13(f), and to determine whether the reporting of entities covered under Section 13(f) is appropriately designed to comply with the statutory requirements. The objectives also included an examination of whether the Commission's policies and procedures for reviewing and processing requests for confidential treatment of information required to be reported under Section 13(f) are adequate and appropriate. In addition, we performed the review to determine whether the oversight over the Section 13(f) process is sufficient.

Overall, our review found that significant improvements could be made with respect to the SEC's review and monitoring of the information reported under Section 13(f). Significantly, our review found that despite congressional intent that the SEC would be expected to make extensive use of the Section 13(f) information for regulatory and oversight purposes, no SEC division or office conducted any regular or systematic review of the data filed on Form 13F. We found that while IM has delegated authority to grant or deny confidential treatment pursuant to Section 13(f), no SEC division or office has been delegated authority to review and analyze the 13F reports, and no division or office considered this task as falling under its official responsibility. Our review found that the information filed on Form 13F could be useful and should be reviewed in a routine and systematic manner.

The OIG's review also disclosed that no SEC division or office monitored the Form 13F filings for accuracy and completeness. As a result, many Forms 13F are filed with errors or problems, which may not be detected or corrected in a timely manner. Because no routine monitoring was conducted, errors or problems with the Form 13F filings were typically detected only in connection with IM's processing of Section 13(f) confidential treatment requests (CTR) or when a member of the public notifies IM of an error in or problem with a Form 13F. Our review also found that there were no checks built into the EDGAR system, through which the Forms 13F are filed, to scan for obvious errors in the forms. Moreover, we found that the current text file format of Form 13F limited the facility to extract, organize, and analyze the data being reported.

In addition, our review disclosed that a third party prepares the official list of Section 13(f) securities that the Commission is required to provide to the public and has been doing so since 1981, based upon specifications received from the SEC in 1979. The official list prepared by the third party was posted to the Commission's website each quarter; however, no SEC division or office conducted any review of the list for accuracy and completeness before it was posted. We believe that such a review is important given that institutional investment managers rely on the official list in preparing their Form 13F reports in accordance with Commission Rule 13f-1. We further found that the SEC had no contract or agreement with the third party with respect to the preparation of the official list of Section 13(f) securities. The lack of a formal contract posed a risk to the SEC that the third party could stop preparing the list at any time, and this informal arrangement appeared to violate the voluntary services prohibition of the Antideficiency Act, 13 U.S.C. § 1342.

The OIG's testing of a sample of CTRs processed by IM revealed that files and supporting documentation could not be located for approximately one-half of the CTRs selected in our initial sample of 25 items. When we selected an additional 12 CTRs, files could not be located for two-thirds of the additional 12 items. The missing files raised concerns that confidential information reported on Form 13F could be inadvertently disclosed. Our testing also indicated that the SEC was not complying with its records retention schedule for CTRs. In addition, our review found that with respect to several CTRs, IM had not rendered a final decision on a timely basis, thus affording certain filers *de facto* confidential treatment of their 13F reports.

Finally, our review disclosed that the current Section 13(f) reporting requirements were outdated and did not currently require disclosure of all significant activities of institutional investment managers, thus rendering the data less useful than they could have been to investors and regulators.

Our review determined that several improvements in the Section 13(f) reporting process were needed to ensure, consistent with Congress's intent in enacting this Section, that useful and reliable data were provided to the public and government regulators. Specifically, we recommended the following:

- The Chairman's Office should delegate primary responsibility for reviewing, analyzing, and monitoring Form 13F information to the appropriate division or office.

- IM and the Office of Information Technology should continue previous efforts to implement checks in the EDGAR system to detect and/or correct obvious errors in Forms 13F and work together to update Form 13F to a more structured format that will make the data easier to extract and analyze.

- The Chairman's Office should assign to an appropriate division and/or office responsibility for reviewing the official list of Section 13(f) securities that is prepared quarterly by a third party and test it on a sample basis.

- IM, in consultation with the Chairman's Office, should take appropriate steps to improve its policies and procedures to ensure that written requests for confidential treatment (particularly certain novel requests) under Section 13(f) are granted or denied within an appropriate timeframe so that filers are not afforded *de facto* confidential treatment as a result of IM not issuing a written response.

- IM, in consultation with the Chairman's Office, should request that the Division of Risk, Strategy, and Financial Innovation update its previous analysis of the impact of increasing the Section 13(f) reporting threshold of $100 million.

- IM, in consultation with OGC, the Office of International Affairs, and the Chairman's Office, should take appropriate steps to improve its policies and procedures to ensure that requests for relief under Section 13(f) made by certain large foreign institutional investment managers are addressed in a timely and appropriate manner.

The SEC Divisions and Offices concurred with all 12 of the recommendations in this report. The OIG's full report can be found on the SEC's website at http://www.sec-oig.gov/Reports/AuditsInspections/2010/480.pdf

Planned Financial Oversight Work Of The SEC OIG

SEC OIG Office of Audits, Report No. 499, Assessment of the SEC's Economic Analyses for Dodd-Frank Act's Rulemaking Initiatives

Dodd-Frank has added significantly to the SEC's workload in requiring the SEC to promulgate more than 100 new rules, create five new offices, and produce more than 20 studies and reports. Dodd-Frank also gives the SEC considerable new responsibilities that will have a significant long-term impact on the agency's workload, including oversight of the over-the-counter derivatives market and hedge fund advisers; registration of municipal advisors and security-based swap market participants; enhanced supervision of NRSROs and clearing agencies; heightened regulation of asset-backed securities; and creation of a new whistleblower program.

In a letter signed by members of the U.S. Senate Committee on Banking, Housing, and Urban Affairs on February 15, 2011, some senators expressed concerns about the economic analyses and cost-benefit assessments being performed by federal financial regulatory agencies for certain rules required under Dodd-Frank. Specifically, these senators stated that they had received comments from members of the public who had performed their own analyses of the rules and identified flaws in the federal financial regulatory agencies' analyses.

On May 4, 2011, the SEC OIG received a formal letter from the U.S. Senate Committee on Banking, Housing, and Urban Affairs requesting that the Inspector General initiate a review of the economic analyses performed by the SEC in connection with rulemaking initiatives under Dodd-Frank. As a result, the SEC OIG, along with the Commodity Futures Trading Commission OIG, the Federal Deposit Insurance Corporation OIG, and the Federal Reserve OIG, was asked to perform a review of the economic analyses being performed by the SEC for rulemakings required under Dodd-Frank. In June 2011, the SEC OIG responded to this request for review of economic analyses conducted.

The SEC OIG also plans to conduct a full audit, which will include further review of the SEC's economic analysis for a sample of Dodd-Frank rulemaking projects to determine if the SEC is performing the required cost-benefit analyses for rulemaking initiatives required under Dodd-Frank in compliance with applicable federal requirements. Specific objectives will also include assessing the adequacy of the public comment process and determining if any improvements or best practices can be implemented in the rulemaking initiative process.

Other Planned Oversight Work

The OIG plans to perform other audit work in connection with its oversight of the SEC and concerns as they apply to the broader financial system. Section 922 of Dodd-Frank requires the Inspector General to conduct a study of the whistleblower protections established under the law and to submit a report on its findings no later than 30 months after the date the law was enacted.

Additional oversight work that the OIG plans to conduct includes a review of the SEC's Office of Minority and Women Inclusion, which was created by Dodd-Frank, to ensure that it is operating in accordance with the legislation, and a review of the SEC's internal organizational structure subsequent to Dodd-Frank implementation to ensure efficiencies and lack of duplication of efforts.

Office of Special Inspector General Troubled Asset Relief Program

Background

The Office of the Special Inspector General for the Troubled Asset Relief Program ("SIGTARP") was established by Section 121 of the Emergency Economic Stabilization Act of 2008 ("EESA") and amended by the Special Inspector General for the Troubled Asset Relief Program Act of 2009 ("SIGTARP Act"). Under EESA and the SIGTARP Act, the Special Inspector General has the duty, among other things, to conduct, supervise, and coordinate audits and investigations of the purchase, management, and sale of assets under the Troubled Asset Relief Program ("TARP") or as deemed appropriate by the Special Inspector General.

SIGTARP's oversight mandate did not end with the October 3, 2010, expiration of the Department of the Treasury's ("Treasury") authorization for new TARP funding. Treasury cannot make new purchases or guarantees of troubled assets, but can still administer existing TARP investments and continue to expend TARP funds previously obligated. Under the authorizing provisions of EESA, SIGTARP sunsets when the Government has sold or transferred all assets acquired under TARP. In other words, SIGTARP will remain "on watch" as long as TARP assets remain outstanding.

Role in Financial Oversight

SIGTARP is committed to vigorous oversight of TARP's unprecedented commitment of billions of taxpayer dollars. SIGTARP's goal is to promote economic stability by assiduously protecting the interests of those who fund the TARP programs - i.e., the American taxpayers. SIGTARP fulfills its oversight role on multiple parallel tracks: auditing various aspects of TARP-related programs and activities; investigating allegations of fraud, waste, and abuse related to TARP programs; coordinating closely with other oversight bodies; and striving to promote transparency in TARP programs. Through ten quarterly reports and 14 completed audits, SIGTARP has brought to light to some of the darkest areas of the financial crisis and the Government's response to it, and has offered 72 recommendations to Treasury to help program effectiveness and protect the taxpayer from losses due to fraud.

SIGTARP's primary law enforcement mission is the swift and robust detection and investigation of those who engage in illegal activities related to TARP, and SIGTARP has already produced outstanding results. When Congress created SIGTARP, it understood that TARP's extraordinary expenditure of taxpayer funds would inevitably attract criminal and other unlawful conduct. Congress assigned SIGTARP with primary responsibility for policing TARP to minimize losses to fraud and to bring to justice those who attempt to profit from TARP unlawfully. SIGTARP takes this mandate seriously, working hard to deliver the accountability the American people demand and deserve. SIGTARP's investigative staff is comprised of dedicated and highly experienced special agents and attorneys who hail from a wide range of Federal agencies. SIGTARP co-chairs the Rescue Fraud Working Group of the President's Financial Fraud Enforcement Task Force. SIGTARP also leverages its resources through partnerships with other Federal, state, and local law enforcement agencies to ensure that justice is done. Similar to the FBI, SIGTARP has the authority to investigate crime, but not to prosecute crime. SIGTARP's investigations are making a difference with substantial results in a remarkably short time frame. As of the drafting of this report, 64 individuals and 18 entities had been charged in criminal or civil actions related to SIGTARP investigations, with 22 individuals criminally convicted. SIGTARP helped prevent over $550 million in taxpayer funds from being lost to fraud, and has assisted in the recovery of over $151 million. With more than 150 ongoing investigations, SIGTARP is committed to stopping ongoing fraud, deterring criminal behavior, and bringing criminals to justice.

Recent, Current or Ongoing Work in Financial Oversight

Applying lessons learned from the extraordinary financial assistance provided by the Government to Citigroup, Inc.

SIGTARP released the audit report "Extraordinary Financial Assistance Provided to Citigroup, Inc." on January 13, 2011.[31] The audit report details the basis for the Government's decision to deem Citigroup to be too systemically significant to be allowed to fail and to provide it with additional Government assistance under the Targeted Investment Program ("TIP") and Asset Guarantee Program ("AGP"). In the audit, SIGTARP found that the conclusion of the various Government actors that Citigroup had to be saved was strikingly ad hoc. While there was consensus that Citigroup was too systemically significant to be allowed to fail, that consensus appeared to be based as much on gut instinct and fear of the unknown as on objective criteria. Given the urgent nature of the crisis surrounding Citigroup, the ad hoc character of the systemic risk determination is not surprising. Nevertheless, the absence of objective criteria for reaching such a conclusion raised concerns about whether systemic risk determinations were being made fairly and with consistent criteria. Such concerns could be addressed at least in part by the development, in advance of the next crisis, of clear, objective criteria and a detailed road map as to how those criteria should be applied.

The Dodd-Frank Wall Street Reform and Consumer Protection Act ("Dodd-Frank Act") charged the Financial Stability Oversight Council ("FSOC") with responsibility for developing the specific criteria and analytical framework for assessing systemic significance. The outcome of the next financial crisis is already being determined by the critical decisions regulators are making today in the Dodd-Frank implementation process. As regulators work to implement the Dodd-Frank Act's reforms, continued oversight will be critical in determining the extent to which the Act ultimately meets its objectives. The integrity of our financial system is still at risk. Indeed, the stakes could not be higher. The following includes SIGTARP's conclusions and lessons learned contained in the Citigroup audit.

Conclusions and Lessons Learned in SIGTARP's Released Audit: "Extraordinary Financial Assistance Provided to Citigroup, Inc."

In November 2008, Citigroup teetered on the brink of failure. Even though it had received $25 billion from TARP's Capital Purchase Program just weeks earlier, it was the subject of a global run on its deposits, its stock was in a nosedive as short sellers sought to profit on the market's perception of its deteriorating condition,

---

31   Office of the Special Inspector General for the Troubled Asset Relief Program (SIGTARP), *Extraordinary Financial Assistance Provided to Citigroup, Inc.* (Jan. 13, 2011) (online at www.sigtarp.gov/reports/audit/2011/Extraordinary%20Financial%20 Assistance%20Provided%20to%20Citigroup,%20Inc.pdf).

and the cost of insuring its debt in the credit default swap market was increasing at an alarming pace compared to its peers. Worried that Citigroup would fail absent a strong statement of support from the U.S. Government, and that such failure could cause catastrophic damage to the economy, then-Treasury Secretary Henry Paulson and then-FRBNY President Timothy Geithner held a series of discussions with FRB Chairman Ben Bernanke, FDIC Chairman Sheila Bair, and then-Comptroller of the Currency John Dugan to discuss bailing out Citigroup. The underlying premise of these discussions was that Citigroup was too systemically significant to be permitted to collapse. According to Chairman Bernanke, it was "not even a close call to assist them."

By late on November 23, 2008, following a frantic few days dubbed by its participants as "Citi Weekend," Citigroup had agreed to a Government proposal that would provide Citigroup a package that included asset guarantees and a $20 billion capital infusion in exchange for preferred shares of Citigroup stock. The essential purpose of the deal, as Secretary Paulson and FRBNY President Geithner later confirmed to SIGTARP, was to assure the world that the Government would not let Citigroup fail. After the deal was announced, the impact on the market's perception of Citigroup was immediate: its stock price stabilized, its access to credit improved, and the cost of insuring its debt declined. Citigroup had been saved, at least for the time being. Just over a year later, Citigroup terminated the guarantee program and repaid the $20 billion of Government-supplied capital.

Citigroup Declared a "Systemic Risk"

By law, FDIC could not participate in the Government's assistance package for Citigroup, which would constitute "open bank assistance,"[32] without a waiver from the Secretary of the Treasury in the form of a Systemic Risk Determination.[33] In order to make this determination, which includes the conclusion that FDIC's normal resolution process "would have serious adverse effects on economic conditions or financial stability,"[34] the Secretary of the Treasury must first receive recommendations from the Board of Directors of FDIC[35] and the Board of Governors of the Federal Reserve, and consult with the President of the United States.

FRB Assesses Citigroup's Systemic Risk

On November 23, 2008, the Board of Governors of the Federal Reserve voted unanimously to recommend to the Secretary of the Treasury that a potential Citigroup failure posed a systemic risk. Chairman Bernanke told SIGTARP that a Citigroup failure "would have been Lehman times two or three in terms of the financial sector and the economy." "This was a view strongly held" at the time, he said. Citigroup was perceived as being interdependent and interconnected with a broad array of different financial institutions both in the U.S. and internationally, and in FRB's view, Citigroup's failure would have implications that reached beyond the bank itself, including serious adverse effects on domestic and international economic conditions and financial stability. Specifically, FRB regulators believed that a Citigroup failure would have destabilized the global financial system by seriously impairing already disrupted credit markets, including short-term interbank

---

32   In an open bank assistance agreement, FDIC provides financial assistance to an operating insured bank or thrift determined to be in danger of closing.

33   12 U.S. Code, section 1823(c)(4); 12 C.F.R. 360.1. The only exception to the "least-cost resolution" requirement is when it is determined that a systemic risk to the financial system exists. 12 U.S. Code, section 1821(c)(4)(G).

34   12 U.S. Code, section 1823(c)(4)(G)(i)(I).

35   The Board of Directors of the FDIC includes the FDIC Chairman, FDIC Vice Chairman, FDIC Director, Comptroller of the Currency, and the Director of the Office of Thrift Supervision.

lending, counterparty relationships in qualified financial contract[36] markets, bank and senior subordinated debt markets, and derivatives.

FDIC Assesses Citigroup's Systemic Risk

On Sunday, November 23, 2008, FDIC's Board of Directors met to consider whether or not to recommend that Treasury invoke the systemic risk exception and allow FDIC to participate in open bank assistance. During this meeting, FDIC staff recommended that the Board find that the failure of Citigroup and its insured affiliate banks and thrifts would have serious adverse effects on domestic and international economic conditions and financial stability.

Based largely on information from Citigroup's primary regulators, FRB and OCC, FDIC's Board of Directors and FDIC staff discussed how Citigroup's failure would seriously and negatively affect already disrupted credit markets, including short-term interbank lending, counterparty relationships, qualified financial contracts markets, and bank and senior subordinated debt markets, and would further disrupt the related markets in derivatives and other products. In addition, they noted in the meeting that Citigroup's failure would have serious consequences for the functioning of the global payment system. Chairman Bair told SIGTARP, "We were told by the New York Fed that problems would occur in the global markets if Citi were to fail. We didn't have our own information to verify this statement, so I didn't want to dispute that with them." During this meeting several concerns were highlighted by FDIC Board members and staff:

- "It's obviously a systemic risk situation. I don't have any question about that," said Office of Thrift Supervision Director John Reich.

- "The risk profile of Citibank[37] is increasing rapidly due to the market's lack of confidence in the company and the substantially weakened liquidity position. Without substantial Government intervention that results in a positive market perception on Monday morning, OCC and Citigroup project that Citibank will be unable to pay obligations or meet expected deposit outflows next week," an FDIC official said.

- "We were on the verge of having to close this institution because it can't meet its liquidity Monday morning," Chairman Bair said. "They have $500 billion in foreign deposits that nobody can guarantee."

- "The issue now is the potential for a large worldwide bank run, and that's what has got to be brought under control," one participant[38] said.

At the end of the November 23, 2008, meeting, the FDIC Board unanimously voted to recommend that Treasury invoke the systemic risk exception for Citigroup. While the vote was unanimous, OTS Director Reich, an FDIC Board member, expressed the concern that there had been "some selective creativity exercised in the determination of what is systemic and what's not," and that there "has been a high degree of pressure exerted in certain situations, and not in others, and I'm concerned about parity." In terms of Citigroup, an FDIC official told SIGTARP that the FDIC directors and other Government entities "made a judgment call." With both recommendations in hand, Secretary Paulson was then able to move forward with the process to invoke the systemic risk exception for Citigroup.

---

36 A qualified financial contract is a type of financial agreement that includes, but is not limited to, securities contracts, forward contracts, repurchase agreements, and swap agreements.

37 Citibank, also known as Citibank, N.A., is the largest of Citigroup's five insured entities.

38 The record of this meeting failed to identify which meeting participant made this statement.

Treasury Determines Citigroup Is a Systemic Risk

On November 21, 2008, Secretary Paulson said, "If Citi isn't systemic, I don't know what is." Secretary Paulson consulted with President Bush about making an emergency Systemic Risk Determination for five Citigroup subsidiary banks, which then authorized FDIC to take appropriate action under the systemic risk exception.

An undated action memorandum for the Secretary discussed Treasury's reasons for supporting the Systemic Risk Determination. According to the memorandum, Citigroup's failure would threaten the viability of creditors and counterparties exposed to the institution, impair the liquidity of even well-capitalized institutions, dislocate the credit markets, and undermine business and household confidence in the broader economy.[39]

SIGTARP's Findings and Conclusions

SIGTARP found that the Government constructed a plan that not only achieved the primary goal of restoring market confidence in Citigroup, but also carefully controlled the overall risk of Government loss on the asset guarantee. Citigroup's initial proposal, which would have had the Government guarantee 100% of $306 billion of troubled assets in return for $20 billion in preferred stock, was summarily rejected. Instead, the Government made a take-it-or-leave-it proposal that required Citigroup to absorb the first $37 billion[40] in losses in the asset pool as well as 10% of any losses in excess of that amount in return for approximately $7 billion in Citigroup preferred stock. The Government's risk of loss, in other words, was dramatically less than it would have been under the Citigroup proposal. Indeed, based on various loss projections, the relevant Government actors – Treasury, FDIC, and FRBNY – believed that Citigroup's initial loss position would render any Government loss unlikely. In the end, Citigroup absorbed all of the losses among the guaranteed assets, which totaled $10.2 billion at the time of the termination of the asset guarantee, far less than Citigroup's "deductible."

As one FRBNY official explained to SIGTARP, the deal was structured to "convinc[e] the skittish market that the Federal Government was taking the risk, even though the risk really remained with Citigroup," because the Citigroup loss position ultimately exceeded anticipated losses. In addition to the asset guarantee, the Government also insisted on a $20 billion capital injection in return for preferred stock, even though Citigroup did not request such an injection. Here, too, the focus was on sending a message to reassure the markets – the Government would not let Citigroup fail.

That the Government drove a particularly hard bargain on behalf of taxpayers was reflected in the reaction of many within Citigroup. Citigroup executives were concerned that the Government's terms were too expensive in light of the assistance provided, and some Citigroup insiders recommended against accepting the proposal. In the end, however, Citigroup accepted the deal, chiefly because of its expected impact on the market's perception of Citigroup's viability.

While the parties announced their preliminary agreement on the framework of the asset pool guarantee on November 23, 2008, they did not finalize the list of assets covered by the guarantee until almost one year later. The eventual selection of assets for inclusion in the pool was driven largely by Government-imposed criteria, the application of which, along with accounting adjustments, led to approximately $100 billion in changes

---

39 Secretary Paulson ratified the actions he took on November 23, 2008, in a written determination he executed on January 15, 2009.

40 This was later raised to $39.5 billion.

from the assets originally proposed by Citigroup. These changes had the effect of reducing the expected loss of the guaranteed asset pool, according to Citigroup's internal calculations, by over $9 billion. As a result, the likelihood that the Government would have to cover losses on the guarantee was reduced even further. As one Citigroup official explained, "We were getting less from the Government for the same pay, [but] we proceeded because we were stuck with the deal."

From the perspective of minimizing taxpayer risk on the asset guarantee transaction itself, the deal with Citigroup looks even better with hindsight. Citigroup did not fail, and the global economy avoided the catastrophic financial collapse that many feared would flow from a Citigroup failure. And while the transactions hardly solved all of Citigroup's problems – just months later the Government was compelled to significantly restructure its ownership interest in a manner that left Treasury as Citigroup's single largest common stockholder – the Government incurred no losses, and even profited on its overall investment in Citigroup by more than $12 billion. Nevertheless, two aspects of the Citigroup rescue bear noting.

First, the conclusion of the various Government actors that Citigroup had to be saved was strikingly ad hoc. While there was consensus that Citigroup was too systemically significant to be allowed to fail, that consensus appeared to be based as much on gut instinct and fear of the unknown as on objective criteria. As Secretary Paulson stated on one of the Citi Weekend conference calls, "If Citi isn't systemic, I don't know what is." FDIC Chairman Bair told SIGTARP that "we were told by the New York Fed that problems would occur in the global markets if Citi were to fail. We didn't have our own information to verify this statement, so I didn't want to dispute that with them." Another FDIC official told SIGTARP that in terms of Citigroup's systemic significance, the FDIC directors and other Government entities "made a judgment call." Citigroup CEO Vikram Pandit summed up the feeling at the time when he told SIGTARP that no one knew what the systemic effects of a Citigroup failure would be, and that no one wanted to find out.

Given the urgent nature of the crisis surrounding Citigroup, the ad hoc character of the systemic risk determination is not surprising, and SIGTARP found no evidence that the determination was incorrect. Nevertheless, the absence of objective criteria for reaching such a conclusion raised concerns. Then-Director of the Office of Thrift Supervision John Reich, at FDIC's Board meeting on November 23, 2008, in which FDIC made its determination to proceed with the Citigroup transactions, observed that there had been "some selective creativity exercised in the determination of what is systemic and what's not," and that there "has been a high degree of pressure exerted in certain situations, and not in others, and I'm concerned about parity." Concerns about "selective creativity" and "parity" could be addressed at least in part by the development, in advance of the next crisis, of clear, objective criteria and a detailed road map as to how those criteria should be applied.

Secretary Geithner told SIGTARP that he believed creating effective, purely objective criteria for evaluating systemic risk is not possible: "What size and mix of business do you classify as systemic?...It depends too much on the state of the world at the time. You won't be able to make a judgment about what's systemic and what's not until you know the nature of the shock" the economy is undergoing. Secretary Geithner also suggested that whatever objective criteria were developed in advance, markets and institutions would adjust and "migrate around them." If the Secretary is correct, then systemic risk judgments in future crises will again be subject to concerns about consistency and fairness, not to mention accuracy. The Dodd-Frank Act created FSOC and charged it with responsibility for developing the specific criteria and analytical framework for assessing systemic significance. That process is under way, with FSOC having invited public comment on those issues. SIGTARP remains convinced that even if some aspects of systemic significance are necessarily subjective and dependent on the nature of the crisis at the time, an emphasis on the development of clear, objective criteria in advance of the next crisis would significantly aid decision makers likely to be burdened by enormous responsibility, extreme time pressure, and uncertain information. Moreover, FSOC must be transparent about how it will apply both objective and subjective criteria to a failing institution, and must seek to gauge the market and adjust the criteria in the event that firms do indeed seek to "migrate around them." Without minimizing the legitimate concerns raised by Secretary Geithner, it is imperative that FSOC not simply accept the adaptability of Wall Street firms to work around regulation, but instead maintain the flexibility to respond in kind.

Second, the Government's actions with respect to Citigroup undoubtedly contributed to the increased moral hazard that has been a direct byproduct of TARP. While the year-plus of Government dependence left Citigroup a stronger institution than it had been, it remained, and arguably still remains, an institution that is too big, too interconnected, and too essential to the global financial system to be allowed to fail. Indeed, a senior FRBNY official told SIGTARP in January 2010 (before the passage of the Dodd-Frank Act), that Citigroup was then still "too big to fail," and that if history repeated itself there is "no question we would do it again... [with] a similar or different program." Citigroup's creditors and counterparties were left largely unscathed by its need for repeated assistance from taxpayers, and the concern voiced by Chairman Bair on February 22, 2009, for the need for management changes "at the top of the house" at Citigroup, arguably was not fully addressed. While there have been notable changes at the board level and some changes in management, some of those in Citigroup's senior management who came to the Government seeking assistance in 2008 remain in place.

When the Government assured the world in 2008 that it would use TARP to prevent the failure of any major financial institution, and then demonstrated its resolve by standing behind Citigroup, it did more than reassure troubled markets – it encouraged high-risk behavior by insulating the risk takers from the consequences of failure. Unless and until institutions like Citigroup are either broken up so that they are no longer a threat to the financial system, or a structure is put in place to assure that they will be left to suffer the full consequences of their own folly, the prospect of more bailouts will potentially fuel more bad behavior with potentially disastrous results. Notwithstanding the passage of the Dodd-Frank Act, which does give FDIC new resolution authority for financial companies deemed systemically significant, the market still gives the largest financial institutions an advantage over their smaller counterparts. They are able to raise funds more cheaply, and enjoy enhanced credit ratings based on the assumption that the Government remains as a backstop. Specifically, creditors who believe that the Government will not allow such institutions to fail may under price their extensions of credit, giving those institutions access to capital at a price that does not fully account for the risk created by their behavior. Cheaper credit is effectively a subsidy, which translates into greater profits, giving the largest financial institutions an unearned advantage over their smaller competitors. And because of the prospect of another Government bailout, executives at such institutions might be motivated to take greater risks than they otherwise would, shooting for a big payoff but with reason to hope that if things went wrong they might still be able to keep their jobs.

The moral hazard effects of TARP in general and the bailouts of Citigroup in particular may eventually be ameliorated by full implementation of the provisions of the Dodd-Frank Act, which was intended in part to address the problem of institutions that are "too big to fail." Whether it will do so successfully remains to be seen, with important work by FDIC, FSOC, and a host of other regulators far from complete. Even after those bodies develop and implement new rules and regulations authorized by the Dodd-Frank Act, which would prohibit some of the benefits received by Citigroup under TARP, taxpayers likely won't know about the extent of their continuing exposure until the next crisis. As Secretary Geithner told SIGTARP in December 2010, with the Dodd-Frank Act, the "probability of failure is reduced because the banks hold more capital. The size of the shock that hit our financial system was larger than what caused the Great Depression. In the future we may have to do exceptional things again if we face a shock that large. You just don't know what's systemic and what's not until you know the nature of the shock. It depends on the state of the world – how deep the recession is. We have better tools now, thanks to Dodd-Frank. But you have to know the nature of the shock."

Secretary Geithner's candor about the difficulty of determining "what's systemic and what's not until you know the nature of the shock," and the prospect of having to "do exceptional things again" in such an unknowable future crisis is commendable. At the same time, it underscores a TARP legacy, the moral hazard associated with the continued existence of institutions that remain "too big to fail." It also serves as a reminder that the ultimate cost of bailing out Citigroup and the other "too big to fail" institutions will remain unknown until the next financial crisis occurs.

Council of Inspectors General on Financial Oversight

Charter

(Adopted October 21, 2010)

Authority

On July 21, 2010, President Obama signed into law the Dodd-Frank Wall Street Reform and Consumer Protection Act (PL 111-203), creating the Council of Inspectors General on Financial Oversight.

Purpose

The Council of Inspectors General shall perform functions that include:

- Provide oversight of the Financial Stability Oversight Council.

- Provide a forum for the discussion of ongoing work of each inspector general who is a member of the Council of Inspectors General.

- Submit annually to Congress and the Financial Stability Oversight Council a report highlighting the concerns and recommendations of each inspector general, with a focus on issues that may apply to the broader financial sector, and a summary of general observations of the Council of Inspectors General, with a focus on measures that should be taken to improve financial oversight.

Membership

The Council of Inspectors General on Financial Oversight is chaired by the Inspector General of the Department of the Treasury. Members of the Council include:

Inspector General of the Board of Governors of the Federal Reserve System

Inspector General of the Commodity Futures Trading Commission

Inspector General of the Department of Housing and Urban Development

Inspector General of the Department of the Treasury, CHAIR

Inspector General of the Federal Deposit Insurance Corporation

Inspector General of the Federal Housing Finance Agency

Inspector General of the National Credit Union Administration

Inspector General of the Securities and Exchange Commission

Special Inspector General for the Troubled Asset Relief Program (until termination of authority)

Substitutions

CIGFO members unable to attend a meeting may send a substitute who is permitted to vote on official matters on behalf of the CIGFO member he/she represents.

Meetings

The Council of Inspectors General on Financial Oversight meets at least once each quarter. More frequent meetings may be held at the call of the Chair. Notice of meetings will be provided to members at least one week prior to the meetings. An agenda, information and materials will be distributed to CIGFO members at least 48 hours in advance of each meeting.

The CIGFO will make all decisions by a majority vote of the voting members currently serving. A quorum of at least five members of the CIGFO must be present to conduct business. The Chair may call for an Executive Session for the discussion of confidential matters. Voting members may not cast votes via proxy.

Minutes will be kept of each CIGFO meeting and all votes of the CIGFO will be recorded in the minutes.

Duties

The Chair will facilitate the conduct of business by the CIGFO, will preside over meetings and business affairs, may call meetings of the CIGFO, prepare plans and agendas for meetings, and ensure the CIGFO meets not less frequently than quarterly. The Chair will also serve as the primary point of contact with the Financial Stability Oversight Council and coordinate CIGFO's oversight activities.

The Vice Chair shall be elected by a majority vote of the CIGFO and shall assume all duties of the Chair in his/her absence.

Conflicts of Interest

Any CIGFO member should notify the Chair and disqualify him/herself from participation in the CIGFO discussion or action on any matter the member has, or may appear to have, a conflict of interest.

Working Groups

Working groups may be convened, by majority vote, to evaluate the effectiveness and internal operations of the Financial Stability Oversight Council. Inspector Generals who are members of the Council of Inspectors General may detail staff and resources to a Working Group to enable it to carry out its duties. Working groups shall submit regular reports to the Council and to the Congress on its evaluations.

Annual Report

The CIGFO shall annually submit to the Financial Stability Oversight Council and Congress a report which includes a section, within the exclusive editorial control of each member of the CIGFO, that highlights concerns and recommendations, with a focus on issues that may apply to the broader financial sector, and a summary of general observations of the CIGFO, with a focus on measures that should be taken to improve financial oversight. The CIGFO will also receive the response of the Financial Stability Oversight Council on its annual report.

Amendments

Amendments to this charter may be made by a majority of the voting members currently serving, on a non-delegable basis.

Council of Inspectors General on Financial Oversight

Guidelines for Establishment and Operation of Working Groups to Evaluate the Financial Stability Oversight Council
(Approved February 3, 2011)

I.   Authority and Purpose

Section 989E(a)(3) of the Dodd-Frank Wall Street Reform and Consumer Protection Act (Dodd-Frank Act, Pub. L. No. 111-203) grants the Council of Inspectors General on Financial Oversight (CIGFO) the authority to convene a working group, by a majority vote, for the purpose of evaluating the effectiveness and internal operations of the Financial Stability Oversight Council (FSOC).

II.   Establishment Procedures

The establishment of a CIGFO Working Group shall be conducted on a case-by-case basis and approved by a majority vote of the CIGFO membership. The voting and quorum rules for establishing a CIGFO Working Group shall be the same as those in the operating charter of the CIGFO. All votes of the CIGFO on whether to approve the establishment of a CIGFO Working Group shall be considered a matter of official business.

CIGFO Working Groups may be proposed by any Inspector General then serving as a member of the CIGFO. Each proposal for an FSOC evaluation shall be made in writing and contain a clearly defined objective and scope. Consistent with the Dodd-Frank Act, each proposed evaluation of the FSOC must be related to the effectiveness and internal operations of the FSOC. Recognizing that proposals may contain varying degrees of complexity, the timing of the CIGFO's vote for approval shall be handled expeditiously at the discretion of the Chair of the CIGFO within 30 calendar days unless a CIGFO member requests additional time to review the proposal, in which case the time for the vote may be extended an additional 15 calendar days. The vote may be taken in person or by email at the discretion of the Chair of the CIGFO.

III.   Composition, Resources, and Leadership

Each Inspector General then serving as a member of the CIGFO may participate in the work of a CIGFO Working Group. To enable the CIGFO Working Group to carry out its duties, the Inspectors General who are members of the CIGFO are authorized to detail staff and resources to a CIGFO Working Group. If the scope of an evaluation to be conducted by a CIGFO Working Group may affect the programs and operations of a particular Inspector General's agency, the Inspector General for that agency shall be given the opportunity to participate in the work of the CIGFO Working Group.

For each CIGFO Working Group established under these Guidelines, one Inspector General from the CIGFO membership shall be designated by the Chair of the CIGFO as the Lead Inspector General. The Lead Inspector General of the CIGFO Working Group will serve as the head of the CIGFO Working Group during the course of the FSOC evaluation and shall be responsible for:

- Presenting regular progress updates on the CIGFO Working Group's operations at each CIGFO quarterly meeting (consistent with section IV, below);

- Ensuring that the evaluation is performed in conformance with applicable standards and guidelines;

- Providing legal counsel, as appropriate, in support of the CIGFO Working Group;

- Ensuring the timely completion of all required reports of the CIGFO Working Group and presenting such reports to the CIGFO for review (consistent with section V, below);

- Ensuring that the CIGFO Working Group's evaluation remain within the clearly defined objective and scope throughout the course of the evaluation (consistent with section II, above); and

- Providing, at the conclusion of the CIGFO Working Group's evaluation, a copy of all final reports, including all key supporting documents, to the Chair of the CIGFO (consistent with section VI, below).

In the event that the Lead Inspector General is an Inspector General other than the Chair of the CIGFO, the responsibilities of the Lead Inspector General shall not be construed as conflicting with the authorities and responsibilities of the Chair of the CIGFO.

IV. Progress Updates

Updates on the progress of an established CIGFO Working Group shall be provided at each quarterly meeting of the CIGFO. More frequent updates may be requested by the Chair of the CIGFO.

V. Reporting

A CIGFO Working Group established under these Guidelines is required to submit regular reports to both the FSOC and the Congress on its evaluations of the FSOC. Any report of the CIGFO Working Group shall not be made unless authorized by a majority vote of the CIGFO. The vote on whether to approve a report shall be handled expeditiously at the discretion of the Chair of the CIGFO within 30 calendar days unless a CIGFO member requests additional time to review the report, in which case the time for the vote may be extended an additional 15 calendar days. The vote may be taken in person or by email at the discretion of the Chair of the CIGFO. The Chair of the CIGFO is authorized to require status reports, including any significant issues or findings to date, from a CIGFO Working Group at any time.

VI. Records Maintenance and Retention

Each Office of Inspector General (OIG) that participates in a CIGFO Working Group shall be responsible for appropriately maintaining, safeguarding, and retaining documentation related to the OIG's involvement in the evaluation, consistent with applicable laws, standards, and guidelines. In addition, as a matter of procedure, at the conclusion of any CIGFO Working Group evaluation, it shall be the responsibility of the Lead Inspector General to transmit a copy of the final report (including all key supporting documents) to the Chair of the CIGFO. These records will be retained and disposed of in accordance with applicable legal and administrative requirements and schedules.

VII. Applicable and Appropriate Laws, Regulations, and Guidance

The operations of all CIGFO Working Groups established under these Guidelines shall conform to the appropriate laws, regulations, standards, and guidance applicable to Inspectors General and the Inspector General community.

VIII. Amendments to Guidelines

These Guidelines may be amended, or additional provisions included, by a majority vote of the CIGFO membership.

www.ingramcontent.com/pod-product-compliance
Lightning Source LLC
Chambersburg PA
CBHW080319290526
45790CB00005B/2102